W9-BGD-322

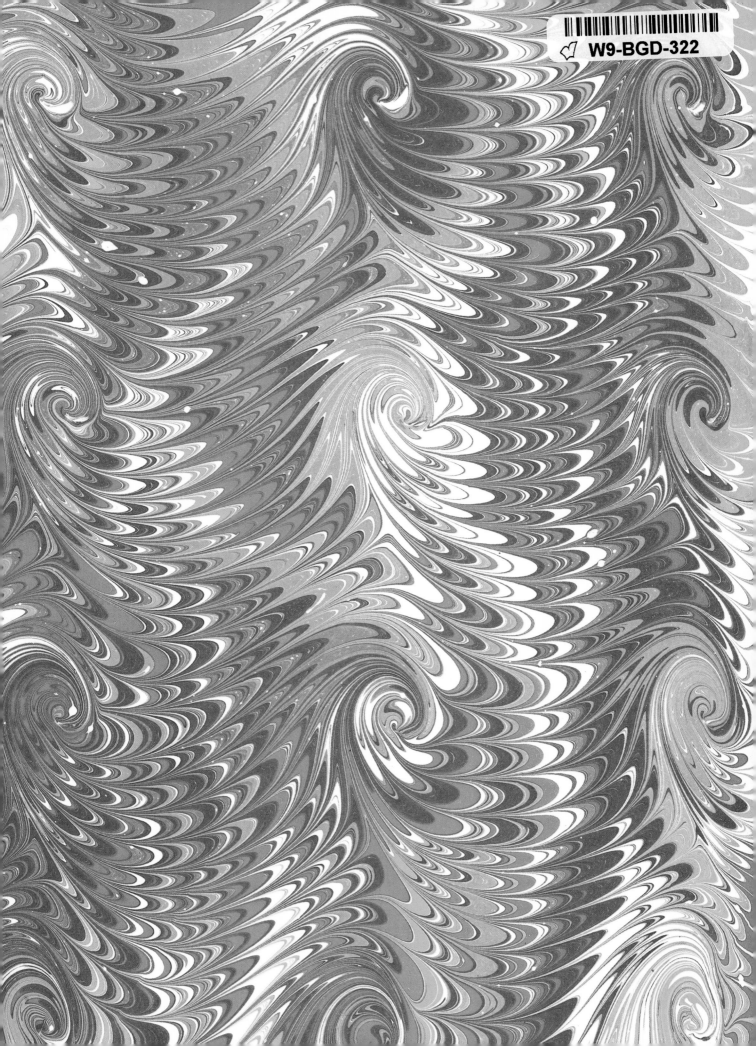

M.C. Smith

THE HOOKER'S ART

Evolving Designs in Hooked Rugs

Jessie Turbayne

Schiffer Publishing Ltd
77 Lower Valley Road, Atglen, PA 19310

This book is dedicated to Michael and Rob.

Published by Schiffer Publishing, Ltd.
77 Lower Valley Road
Atglen, PA 19310
Please write for a free catalog.
This book may be purchased from the publisher.
Please include $2.95 postage.
Try your bookstore first.

We are interested in hearing from authors
with book ideas on related subjects.

Copyright © 1993 by Jessie A. Turbayne.
Library of Congress Catalog Number: 93-85274.

All rights reserved. No part of this work may be reproduced or used in any forms or by any means—graphic, electronic or mechanical, including photocopying or information storage and retrieval systems—without written permission from the copyright holder.

Printed in the United States of America.
ISBN: 0-88740-459-6

Acknowledgements

To all who contributed to the making of this book I express my respect and gratitude. Involved in the undertaking were family members, friends and associates, rug hookers and teachers, antique dealers, gallery and auction house owners, churches, schools and museums. A special word of appreciation to Virginia Hall, Ramona Maddox, Annie Spring, Naomi Stopher and Mary Paul Wright, hooked rug enthusiasts all. To Michael, Susan and Joan, words of thanks for your support throughout this project. And to Nancy Schiffer and Schiffer Publishing, my deepest gratitude for making the job of writing this book a pleasure.

Kind acknowledgements to: Dot Abbott, Marni Agnew, Dorothea Allen, The Ascension Lutheran Church, Charlotte, North Carolina; Gladys Badger, Barbara Ham Bancroft, Janet Bandilli, Grace H. Barker, Charles G. Barnes, Corinne Barry, Beauport-Sleeper, McCann House, Gloucester, Massachusetts; Roland Beliveau, Pat Berry, Dede Bowles, Ida Bowman, Bristol Auctioneers, Boston, Massachusetts; Ethel Bruce, Mildred Buerkel, Mary Sheppard Burton, The Canadian Consulate, Boston, Massachusetts; Lou Carson, Castle In The Clouds Rug Hooking School, Chattanooga, Tennessee; Pamela J. Chase, The Chattanooga's Hookkrafters, Betsy Adams Church, Harriett Claridge, Phyllis Clukay, Mary Lu Cole, Douglas Congdon-Martin, Mary Ellen Cooper, Laura Coppinger, Covenant College, Chattanooga,Tennessee; Louise Covington, Barbara Cox, Kathleen Crowe, S. Culler, Larayne Cunningham, Jane Curtin, W. Cushing and Company, Kennebunkport, Maine; Marion Darbe, Beverly J. Darling, Salma S. Dhanji, Daryl T. Dobson, Colette Donovan, Newburyport, Massachusetts; C.M. Edwards, Jeanne Edwards, Nancy Elliot, Mary Evans, Jeanne Fallier, Charlotte Farr, The First Christian Church, Chattanooga, Tennessee; First Ward Elementary School, Charlotte, North Carolina; Ethel Fitzgerald, Connie Fletcher, Pat Fletcher, Mary Floyd, Forager House Antiques, Nantucket Island, Massachusetts and Washington, Pennsylvania; Norma Frazier, Jack Gantos, Georgia Department of Natural Resources Parks and Historic Sites Division, Chiz Gilbert, Sandy Gilliam, Faye A. Gilman, Carol Gjertsen, Alan Goldstein and Judith Taylor/Fine Art, Fine Rugs, Point Pleasant, Pennsylvania; Celia Gutting, Jacqueline Gutting, Fumiyo Hachisuka, Hallie H. Hall, Marion N. Ham, Jacqueline L. Hansen, Scarborough, Maine; Mary E. Hargrove, Pat Haviland, Sandy

A rug in the making. Carolyn Watt has hooked a likeness of her Nantucket home using hand-dyed and as is wool material.

Jane Hubbard designed and hooked a mat to be placed on the lid of a degamalon. The antique Oriental instrument is used in the Hubbard's living room as a coffee table. 1991. *Photo courtesy of Jane Hubbard*

Heino, Faith Henshall, Doris Hettler, Eva Holmes, John and Vida Holmes, Jane Hubbard, Peg Irish, Esther Jackson, Faye Jackson, Jean Jones, Carol Kassera, Nancy Kelly, Martha Kendrick, Pat and Connie Kent, The Kent Collection, Prince Edward Island, Canada, Georgia Kimball, Robert H. Kurtz, Irma Lampert, Ann Lawrence Antiques, New York, New York; John and Meredith LeBeau, Nan Lee, Diane Legros, Little White House, Warm Springs, Georgia; Celia Lockerman, Dan Loffler, Roslyn Logsdon, Dot Loney, Anne Lower, Earl C. Majors, Betty Maley, Mary Mann, Rowena Marin, Rosemarie Martell, Martin House Farm, Swansea, Massachusetts; Nancy Martin, Myrna Mason, The Massachusetts Society of the Colonial Dames of America, Betty McClentic, Lita McCormick, Polly McGuire, Betty McHugh, Tom McMillan, Wendy Meredith, The Mills-Mosseller Studio, Tryon, North Carolina; Linda Molloy, Susan Morin, Robert and Joan Moshimer, Ronald Mosseller, Mary Brandt Murphy, Elsie Myserian, Ruth B. Nagel, Norman and Ruth Nau, Marjorie Noon, Maria R. O'Brien/Antiques and Interiors, Marblehead, Massachusetts; Grace N. O'Neil, Rita O'Neil, Cheryl Orcutt, Peterborough, New Hampshire; Helen Payne, John Pence Gallery, San Francisco, California; Mary Perry, Phyllis Perry, Shirley H. Perry, Muriel Peveril, Mary E. Philbrick, Pine Cone Antiques, Haverhill, New Hampshire; Margaret Pinkham, Prince Edward Island Musem and Heritage Foundation, Barbara Pritle, Quail Hill Designs, Brunswick, Maine; Mary Carden Quinn, Floral Park, New York, Ralph A. Ridolfino, Ocean City, New Jersey; Jean Crockett Ritchie, Ruth Roccia, Bert and Carol Rosengarten, Elizabeth Rowe, Priscilla Ruegg, The Rugging Room, Westford, *Rug Hooking*, Harrisburg, Pennsylvania; Mildred Sacco, Salma's Selections, Fort Lauderdale, Florida; Janine Denizard Saint-Louis, Susan E. Schaefer, Jane Schultz, Stephen Score Inc., Essex, Massachusetts; Richard L. Scott, Virginia Sheldon, John Smidt Company, Peabody, Massachusetts; Susan L. Smidt, Pamela J. Smith, Annie A. Spring, The Society for the Preservation of New England Antiquites, Boston, Massachusetts; Betty Supple, Marjorie Stafford, Sue Stopher, Catherine Taff, Barbara Tarr, Donna A. Terzian, Salem, Massachusetts; Cindy Thompson, Thomas M. Thompson Antiques, Northfield, New Hampshire; Mary MacLaren Thomson,

Tiffany and Company, Boston, Massachusetts; Pat Tritt, C. Allan Turbayne, Evelyn N. Turbayne, James A. Turbayne, Stephen A. Turbayne, Wendy Ullmann, Sandy Vohr, Judith Walcott, Christine Waters, Carolyn Watt, Susan Scott Webb, Theresa Wells, Wenham Cross Antiques, Boston, Massachusetts; Angela Wescott, Janet West, John West, Sandy Wilder, Mary Williamson, Beth Wilson, Ann Winterling, Garth Winterling, Mary Irma Worley, Richard and Ellen Youlden, Gayle M. Young.

Rug measurements have been rounded to the nearest inch. Those hooked rugs, mats and related items to which no acknowledgement has been ascribed belong to the author.

The small painting on board was purchased by the author at a yard sale for ten cents. For years it sat on the kitchen shelf. Friend and fellow hooker Dot Abbott borrowed the scene and for Christmas presented me with the painting and its hooked stool companion. 1991. Stool top measures 10″ x 20″.

"Optical Illusion,"designed and hooked by Jeanne Fallier.
Diameter 36". *Photo courtesy of Jeanne Fallier*

Table of Contents

Mary Hargrove hooked a back and seat covering for a Victorian chair. 1990.

Introduction

Anthony and Florence come to visit more often. Perhaps my enthusiasm and love for hooked rugs is contagious. Anthony has started to hook folk art pieces. All the rugs, whole and full of holes, of varying ages, shapes and sizes that once filled our overcrowded home now reside in a newly built studio. The reclaimed living quarters could account for the frequent social calls of our friends the Travises. But conversations always turn to hooking and we feel most comfortable in the room where the rugs, whole and full of holes, are piled, rolled and stacked.

Much has changed in my life since the publication of *Hooked Rugs/ History and the Continuing Tradition*. I have still not become accustomed to people requesting my autograph. Prior to the book being printed, the only things I was asked to sign were checks and school permission slips. It has all been quite marvelous. Letters, photographs, telephone conversations and personal visits have put me in touch with more antique dealers, collectors and rug hookers than I ever could have imagined. My knowledge about the subject of hooked rugs has once again been enriched and my list of friends lengthened.

The inspiration for this book came from an invitation Michael and I received to address the many rug hookers living in the southeastern part of the United States. Throughout our travels we experienced true Southern hospitality and had the priviledge of viewing some of the finest hooked rugs being made today. The South may not have as lengthy a tradition of hooked rug history as the northeastern United States and the Maritime Provinces of Canada, but this text features many Southern hooking artists and will dispel any notions that rugs are hooked only in the regions where snow falls all winter.

Too often are hooked rugs perceived merely as small, scatter-size floor coverings crafted by those of modest means. My research and the pages that follow put such misconceptions to rest.

In reading this book and sharing these photographs I trust my readers will become more appreciative of hooked rugs, and through this appreciation will regard rug hooking as an art.

Jessie A. Turbayne

Jean Crockett Ritchie enjoys hooking a woodland scene. Each of her three children help in selecting the colors of wool she hooks.

1 Welcome Mats

The half-moon or semicircle is a versatile hooked rug. Placed at a doorway, it invites all to enter, frequently welcoming visitors with the written word. The hand-hooked mats add touches of color to any entranceway. Often the rug bears the name of those who dwell within. Nautical scenes, fruits, flowers and geometric patterns, landscapes and portraits of humans and animals; all have been depicted on threshold mats.

These charming half-moon shaped hooked rugs are equally at home when displayed before a chest, bureau or hearth.

A welcome mat upon the entrance floor
beckons me through my home's front door.
Old friend hooked from worn garments of those
who brightened my days, who caused deep woes.
Nothing more than burlap, wool and rag
yet every time I tend to lag.
And remember ones I long to see;
they who meant so much to me.
Little rug laying still and flat
who would think you could do all that?

A threshold rug from the collection of Ralph W. Burnham. Mr. Burnham, an Ipswich, Massachusetts antique dealer, was responsible for popularizing the use of hooked rugs as a decorating element beginning in the early 1900s. Frost pattern. Circa 1900. 26" x 40". *Courtesy of Annie A. Spring*

"Hooked Rug Magnate," Ralph W. Burnham described this hooked mat as "a very dainty threshold rug for use in a chamber. Border—blue. Field—white. Basket—blue tones. Flowers—natural colors. This is a little wonder." Hooked of yarn. 1925. *Courtesy of Annie A. Spring*

Three roses in full bloom bid welcome to arriving guests. Note the unusual buds with finger-like petals. Frost pattern. Circa 1930. 31" x 51". *Courtesy of Joan Moshimer. Photo by Robert Moshimer.*

A single rose and two large buds are framed by triangles of red and a bold banner proclaiming WELCOME. The addition of a series of braids protect vulnerable edges of the hooked rug, increasing its longevity and dimensions. Circa 1890. 23" x 43". *Private Collection*

A garland of skillfully shaded roses and buds grace this modern hooked rug. 22" x 36" *Courtesy of Beth Wilson and Polly McGuire*

Simple hooked mat of primary colors. 1930-1940.18"x26". *Courtesy of Wenham Cross Antiques*

A delightful bouquet of poppies and pansies designed and hooked by Jacqueline L. Hansen in 1988. 21" x 45".

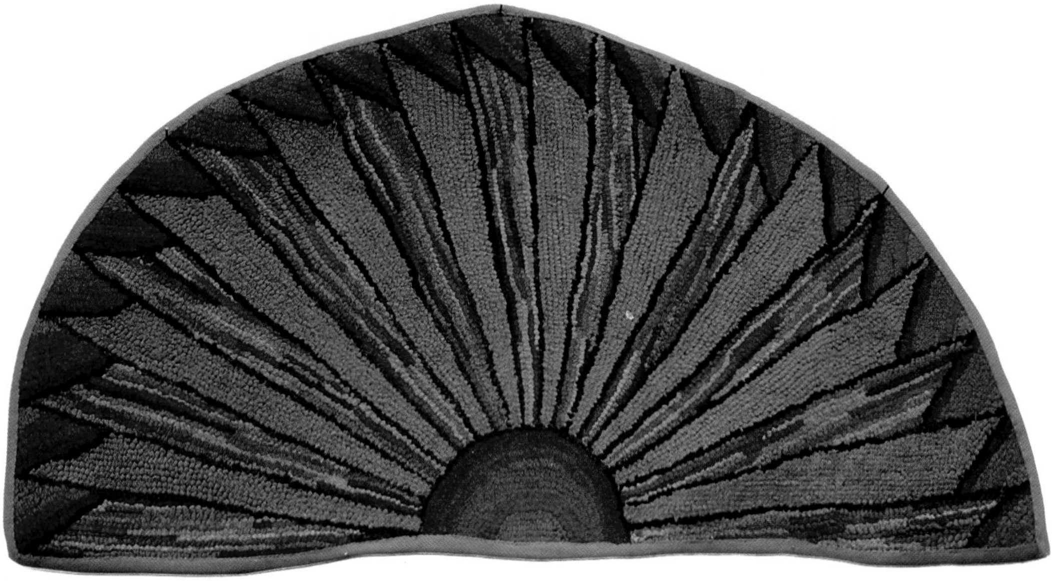

The owner has dubbed this mat his "buzz saw" rug, since the design resembles a saw mill blade. He describes its vintage as "early logging camp." Originally a full circle, the rug most likely was cut in half due to wear. Circa 1920. 19" x 36". *Private Collection*

A welcome mat of ship and lighthouse from the du Pont Estate on Long Island, New York. Circa 1900. 26" x 33". *Courtesy of Forager House Collection*

Recalling another era, three luxury liners of graduated proportions sail under full steam. Hooked in the 1950s. *18" x 33". Private Collection*

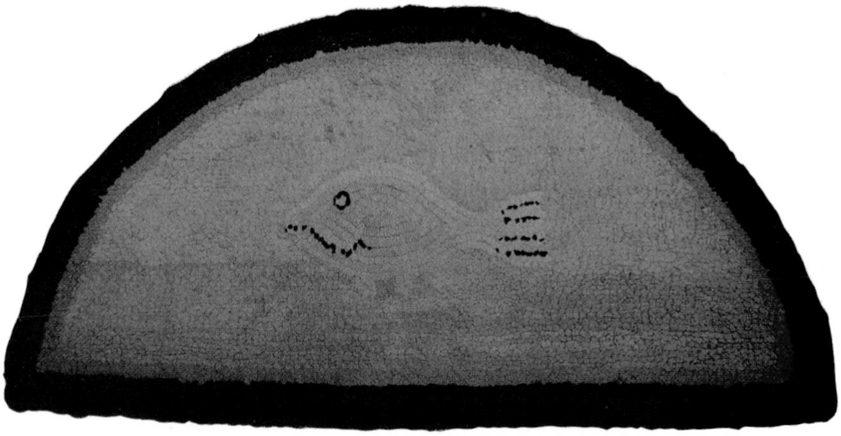

A whimsical fish with mouth almost half the size of its body swims alone on a hooked ocean of blue. Circa 1940. 18" x 36". *Courtesy of Priscilla J. Ruegg*

This grouping of shells indigenous to warm sea waters was designed and hooked by Jeanne Fallier in 1990. 23" x 40". *Photo courtesy of Jeanne Fallier*

A smiling whale tosses the occupant of an airborne dory as fellow sailors row by. Modern reproduction of an 19th century rug. Hooked by C. M. Edwards. 24″ x 40″. *Photo courtesy of C. M. Edwards*

Mother cat watches as her kitten plays with a ball of yarn. Hooked of woolen yarn. From the collection of Ralph W. Burnham. Circa 1910. 28″ x 40″. *Courtesy of Annie A. Spring*

Guests must cross the path of this black cat before entering the house. Designed by Sharon Gilman. Recently hooked by Faye A. Gilman. *Photo courtesy of Faye A. Gilman.*

Striped cat with golden eyes prowls amidst strawberry fruits and flowers. 1980s. *Courtesy of Wenham Cross Antiques*

Stars, stripes and the American eagle were proudly placed at the threshold by a patriotic rug hooker. Pearl K. McGown pattern. 1950-1960. 20" x 33". *Courtesy of Maria R. O'Brien/ Antiques and Interiors*

Jacqueline L. Hansen hooked a likeness of her 1840 home in Scarborough, Maine. 1991. 23" x 35".

Rug hooking became a popular cottage industry during the first half of the twentieth century. This rug was purchased from the Dennison Company of Portland, Maine. While visiting the company workshop in the early 1950s, the owner of this custom-made mat recalls seeing many women seated at a long table busily hooking rugs. Hooked from woolen yarn. 1950s. 21" x 35". *Courtesy of Wenham Cross Antiques*

"Golden Fruit," a design by Joan Moshimer, was recently hooked by Larayne Cunningham. 25" x 41". *Photo by Jeanne Edwards*

An Oriental fan served as a model for this modern semicircle rug hooked by Catherine Taff. *Photo courtesy of Catherine Taff*

Early tapestries embroidered with woolen yarns inspired the design of this threshold rug. "Crewel Crescent" is a Joan Moshimer pattern. 1970s. 24" x 41". *Photo courtesy of Virginia Sheldon*

The rugs woven in the Persian city of Kashan were and continue to be of the finest quality. Traditional colors have changed over the years. Most recently the carpets are worked in pale pastel shades. Carol Gjertsen chose to hook "Kashan," a design by Jane McGown Flynn, using a five-colour Kashan palette. 28" x 44". *Photo by Jeanne Edwards*

Though the semicircle is most popular, welcome mats are worked in varying shapes and sizes. Virginia Hall hooked this chevron pattern in 1988. The design was adapted from an antique rug. 24" x 35".

An oval welcome mat depicting her cherished home was designed and recently hooked by Faye Jackson. Weeping willows flank the house. Note the furry friend atop a checkerboard roof. 22" x 30". *Photo courtesy of Faye Jackson*

2 Runners

A hand-hooked runner transforms an unadorned flight of stairs into an artist's gallery. Each step is a showplace for the rug hooker's work in wool; colorful paintings of rag that cushion well-traveled treads and cascade down risers. The runner's design can be a continuous pattern, or the risers and treads can portray different themes.

Stair runners are a hooking project of grand proportions; requiring much time and materials. The long rug is worked upon burlap, linen or other suitable foundation in an unbroken length for a tread and riser combination, or in separate pieces for each tread and riser. The length and width varies according to the stairway. An average flight of stairs in a home [12 steps] requires a rug of approximately 20 to 25 feet in length. Runners can be hooked for a straight stairway or fashioned to accommodate the twists and turns of a more elaborate structure.

The demand for hooked runners by collectors and interior decorators exceeds the supply. Their charm is evident to all who view them.

Ralph W. Burnham offered the pattern for this hooked stair runner in his catalog of January 15, 1937. The repeating design of two large roses surrounded by leaves rested upon the treads and each riser showcased the varying folk art scenes. *Courtesy of Annie A. Spring*

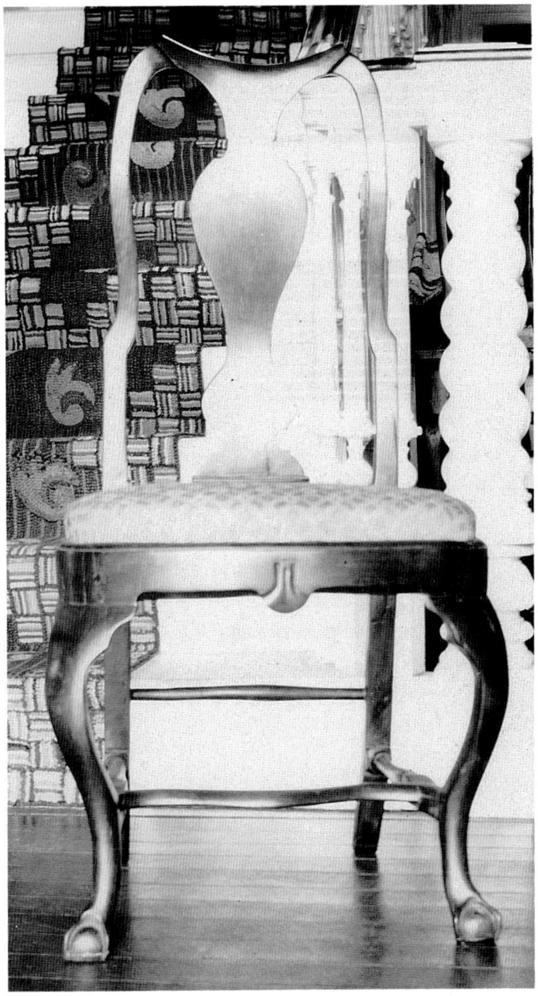

When advertising furniture, antique dealer Ralph W. Burnham used the opportunity to display a few hooked rugs. A runner of geometric and scroll pattern cascades down the stairway. Photo taken during the 1920s. *Courtesy of Annie A. Spring*

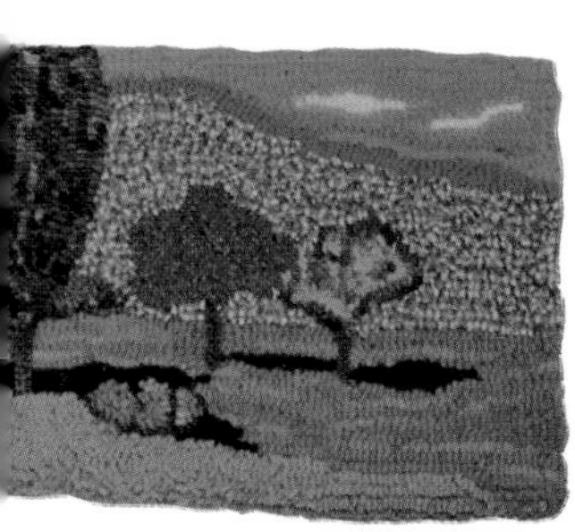

This series of hooked stair risers depict scenes surrounding the home of John Greenleaf Whittier, Mount Cachmacura, New Hampshire. Hooked in Epson, New Hampshire during the 1930s. Each riser is 8″ x 24″. *Courtesy of Ann Lawrence*

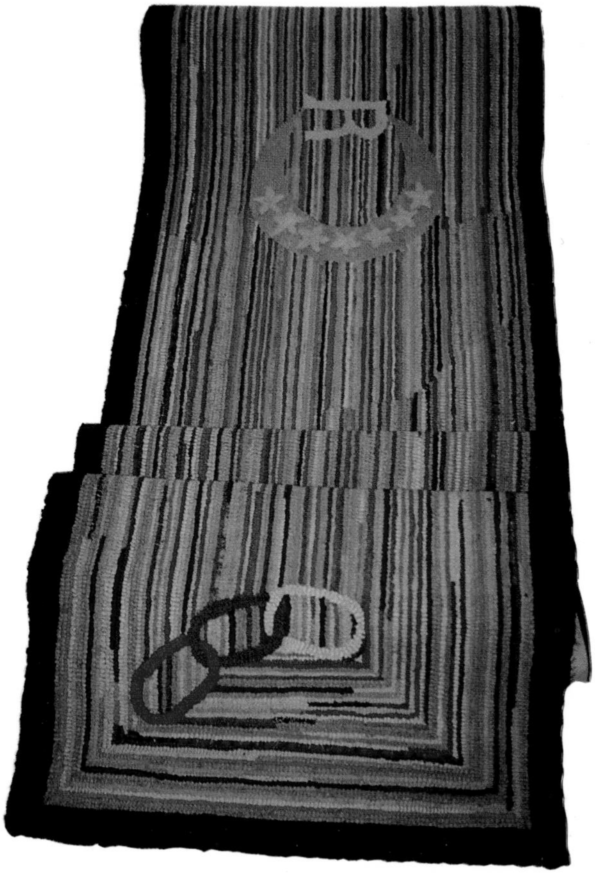

The Independent Order of Odd Fellows was created in England during the second quarter of the eighteenth century. The Grand Lodge formed in England in 1803 and shortly after became organized in the United States. The Rebekah degree for women was established in 1851. The runner pictured combines symbols of both organizations and was most likely hooked by the ladies of the Rebekah Lodge. Made in Nova Scotia. Circa 1940. 26″ x 14′ 4″ *Information and rug courtesy of the Kent Collection*

WELCOME

A greeting of WELCOME suggests this runner was placed on stairs opposite an entrance door. The runner, hooked in several sections of different lengths, was made to accommodate a turning stairway. Scenes of sailboats, beaches, woodlands, village houses, churches and people show changing seasons. A colorful hit or miss pattern served to cushion the tread. Hooked by a woman from the South Shore area of Massachusetts. 1940-1950.

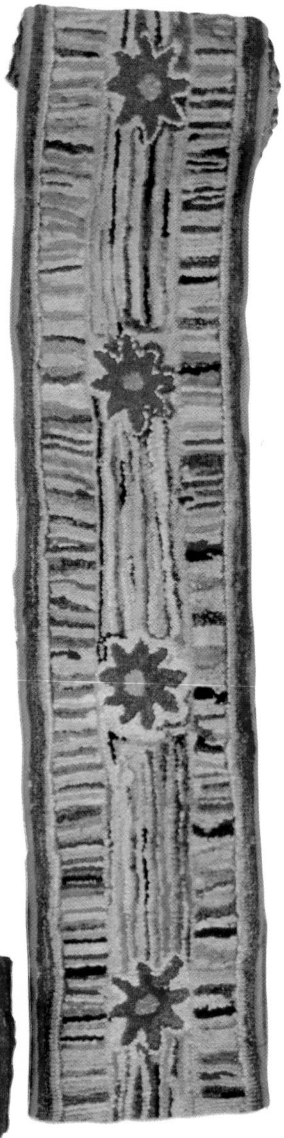

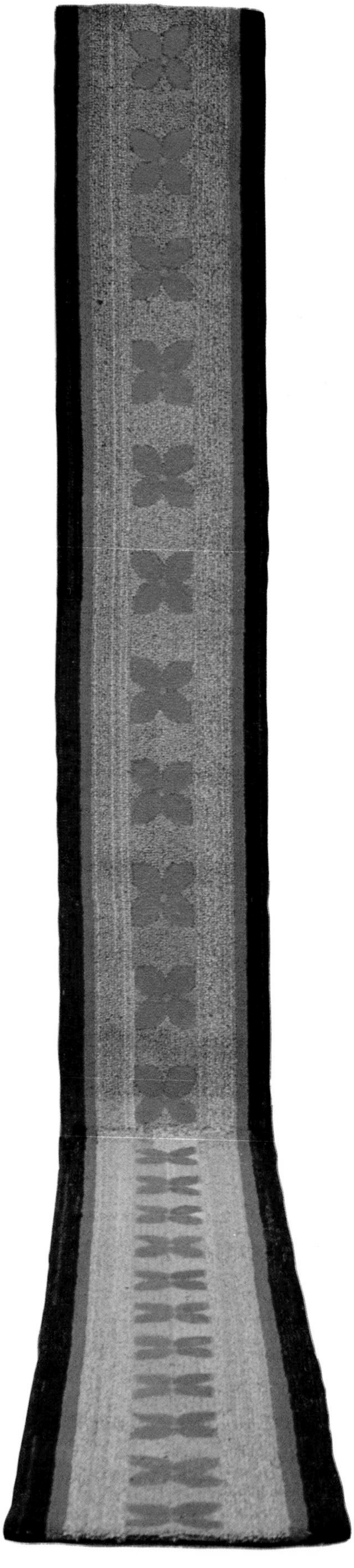

A simple pattern of colorful leaves makes a charming stair runner. From a farmhouse in Jefferson, Texas. Hooked of wool fabric. Circa 1940. 31" x 17' 8". *Collection of Anne Lower and Jack Gantos*

The rug maker that hooked this narrow runner used a variety of textiles, including cotton calico, linen, flannel, paisley and woolen yarns. Circa 1890. 13" x 16' 11". *Private Collection*

A simple runner hooked entirely from three colors; varying tones of black, mottled hues of grey and two shades of orange. Circa 1940.

Leon Badger started hooking in the 1950s and continued until his death in 1971. He purchased eight patterns for a stairway runner and designed the others he needed to cover the remaining steps. I had the great pleasure of meeting his wife, Gladys, who passed away in her 99th year. Mrs. Badger told me of the joy her husband, who was self taught, found in hooking this runner. Events that altered the course American history are depicted on each riser. *Courtesy of Gladys Badger and Jane Schultz*

How to Make a Rug

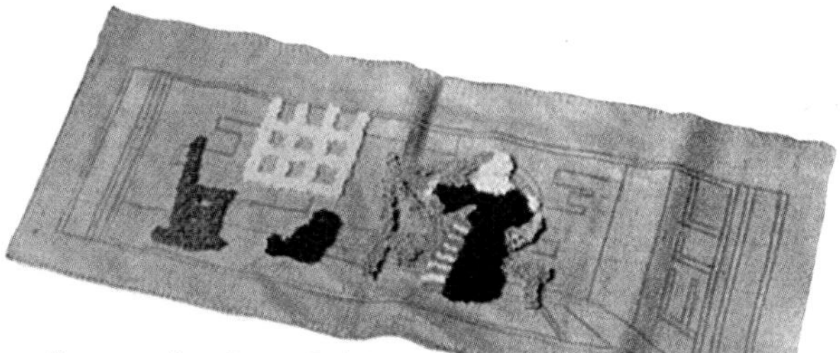

Always outline design first. If you do not use a frame, start in center of rug so burlap will be easier to handle. Fill in design, shading properly. Keep all loops same height

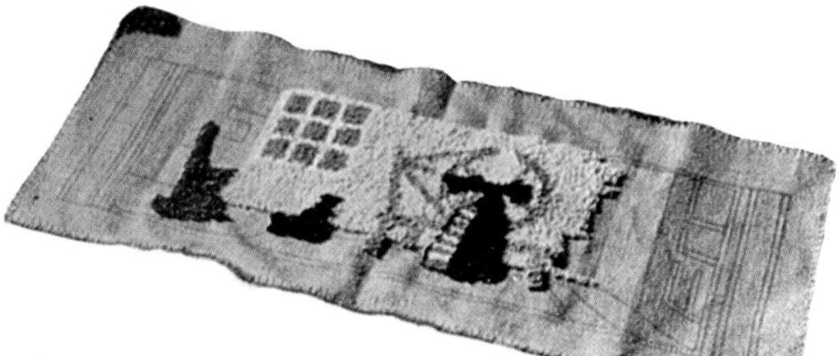

After all outlined designs are completed fill in background, going around individual designs, then filling in between. Treads are varicolored in hit-or-miss pattern. Runner has tricolor border on sides

762 **Completed riser design shown as part of hooked stair runner made by Mrs. Anne B. Clark from our Pattern 762, 70¢. Riser with dates is not included in pattern. This is Mrs. Clark's own house**

Designs and illustrations by Margaret W. Buck

AMERICAN HOME PATTERN NO. 762
American history hooked stair runner, 70¢

FIRST STEAMBOAT

PAUL REVERE'S RIDE

(American Home Pattern 762). Series includes the following motifs—"The Mayflower," "John Smith and Pocahontas," "Spinning Wheel and Colonial Dame," "Paul Revere's Ride," "Spirit of 1776," "Liberty Bell," "The American Eagle," and "First Steamboat." The two motifs especially intended for repeats are Liberty Bell and American Eagle which can be alternated with the other motifs depending on the number of steps to be covered. If staircase had twelve steps you would alternate a bell or eagle between events.

The page from *American Home* magazine that inspired Leon Badger and others to hook a patriotic runner. *Courtesy of Ruth B. Nagel*

Phyllis Perry had only a few lessons when she decided to hook a lengthy stair runner. With the encouragement of her teacher, advice from other rug hookers and the aid of her duck hunting husband and his friends the runner came to life. Hooked on monk's cloth. Completed 1991. 27" x 24'. *Photo courtesy of Phyllis Perry*

A hooked blanket of autumn leaves cushions the tread. *Photo courtesy of Phyllis Perry*

Eva Holmes chose a crewel pattern for the runner she hooked in 1965. Her initials and date are hooked into the riser on the bottom step. *Photo courtesy John and Vida Holmes*

The names of family members and important dates are hooked into the stair runner designed and worked by Eva Holmes. *Photo courtesy of Eva Holmes*

Twisted leafy vines carry salmon hued blossoms and buds up and down this flight of stairs. Hooked by Gladys I. Buerkel, completed in 1951. *Private Collection*

Norma Frazier of Tennesse works diligently on "Plume Leaf," an Heirloom pattern. Finished size 27" x 9'. *Photo courtesy of Norma Frazier*

Cheryl Orcutt of Peterborough, New Hampshire is one of the few individuals that will custom design and hook large rugs on a commission basis. Pictured is the stair runner she designed to coordinate with the acorn finials that decorate her cliente's stairway. The rug was hooked entirely from new wool material except for the recycling of an old coat given to Cheryl by the family that commissioned the work. Cheryl hand dyed all the colors and hooked the rug upon a linen foundation. She began to work the day after Thanksgiving in 1991. The runner was installed on July 20, 1992. 26″ x 21′. *Photos courtesy of Cheryl Orcutt*

3 Grand Proportions

Hooked rugs are generally thought to be scatter-size, color-filled rectangles of handiwork that dot the floors of modest homes. The majority of hand-hooked rugs are indeed small. Rug makers in the past and those who continue the tradition most often choose projects of a manageable scale, drawing designs upon burlap or purchasing printed patterns that yield a completed rug of 2′ x 3′, 3′ x 5′ or similar measurements. Rugs of small size do not require tremendous amounts of wool or rag to work with; they are easily carried about while in progress, and when they are finished they become a decorating asset. All rug hooking is time consuming. Scatter-size hooked rugs are more likely to be completed than undertakings of overwhelming dimension.

There are a few dedicated hookers who do create floor coverings on a large scale, though, devoting years of work to one rug. With abundant perseverance, individual women and men have hooked rugs of grand proportions; masterpieces that would cover the expansive marble floor in a Newport, Rhode Island summer mansion. A rug hooking project of sizable measurement [8′ x 10′, 9′ x 12′ or larger] demands planning, skill, time and great quantities of rag to hook with.

Rug makers must consider dimensions of the room where the rug will be placed. The scale of the design should be appropriate for the area and its decor. Big rugs require custom made patterns that are ordered from commercial suppliers or made at home by sewing pieces of burlap, linen or cotton rug warp together. The design is stenciled or drawn freehand on the burlap or other foundation.

Once the pattern is readied, large quantities of hooking textiles must be gathered. Rugs are fashioned from discarded clothing, blankets, rags and at times cotton or woolen yarns. The preferred hooking material is 100% wool fabric. Rug hookers often recycle wool clothing or purchase wool fabric by the yard. It takes approximately four square feet of wool to hook one square foot of rug.

Ralph W. Burnham, antique dealer and proprieter of the Ipswich, Massachusetts Trading Post, was responsible for promoting hooked rugs as a decorating asset from the early 1900s until his death in 1938, His clientele list was extensive and impressive. Burnham placed hooked rugs in some of the most elegant homes in America. *Courtesy of Annie A. Spring*

Experience has taught that it is best to over-estimate the amount of material needed to complete a rug. The greatest fear of any rug maker is to run out of an unobtainable tweed, plaid or subtly dyed background wool before a rug is completed. Homes of devoted rug hookers are filled with bulging boxes, barrels and bags of wool rags waiting to worked into a project. Though shared, swapped and sold among fellow ruggers, hookers horde more rag than they will ever use in their life time. Better to have a little extra material than not enough! Leftovers can always be used in another rug.

Some choose to hook their gathered fabrics as is; others dye the materials to desired colors. Then the wool and/or rag material is cut into thin strips. Generally the width of the strip is uniform throughout the rug. Hookers may cut their material to a spaghetti-like 3/32" or to a width of 2". The length varies. Strips are cut with scissors or sliced by a hand cranked or machine run cutter manufactured specifically for rug hooking purposes. The cutter saves time and wear and tear on the rug hooker, but in no way determines the quality of the finished rug.

With a pattern prepared, color scheme planned and fabric readied for use, the time consuming labor of hooking begins. Using a simple tool that resembles a short crochet hook set in a handle, the tiny holes formed from the burlap's weave are painstakingly filled with loops hooked from the cut strips of fabric. It may take several hours to complete a six inch square area of rug. The more detailed a design and the thinner the strips are sliced, the longer the hooking process will take.

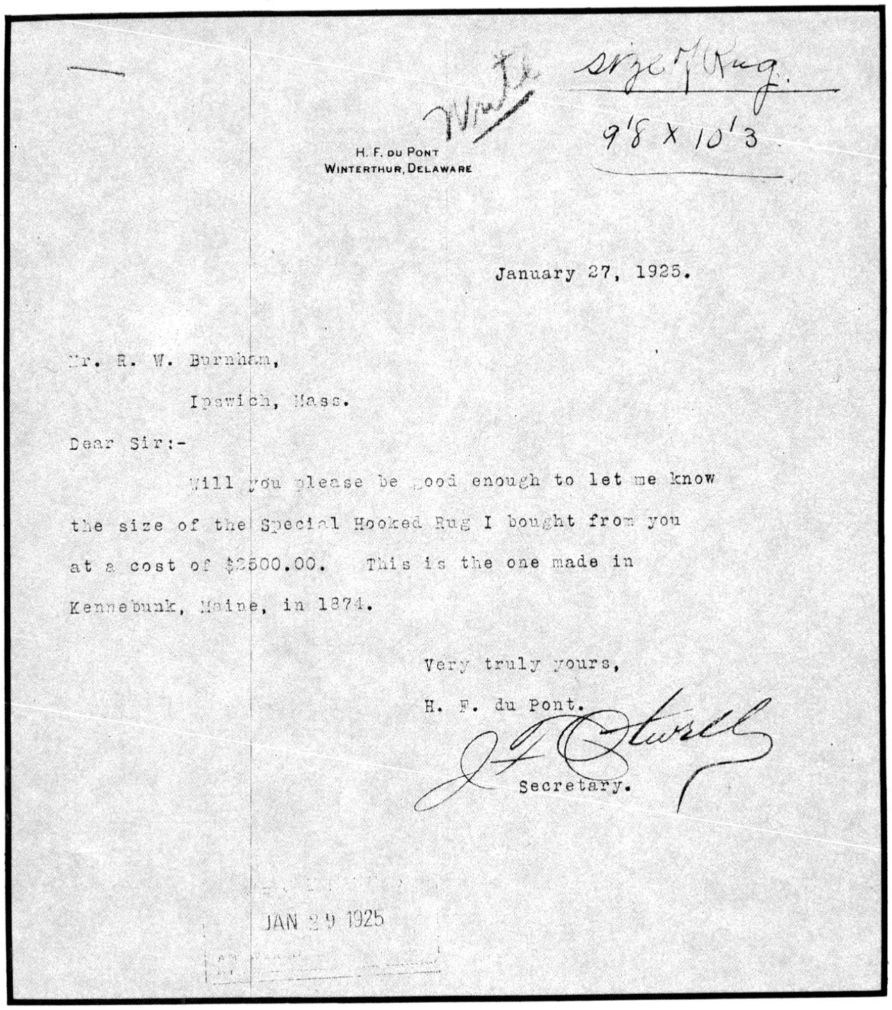

Size of Rug
9'8 X 10'3

H. F. du Pont
Winterthur, Delaware

January 27, 1925.

Mr. R. W. Burnham,
Ipswich, Mass.

Dear Sir:-

Will you please be good enough to let me know the size of the Special Hooked Rug I bought from you at a cost of $2500.00. This is the one made in Kennebunk, Maine, in 1874.

Very truly yours,
H. F. du Pont.
Secretary.

JAN 29 1925

An inquiry to Mr. Burnham from H. F. du Pont's secretary. The rug in question measured 9' 8" x 10' 3" (as noted in the upper right hand corner of the letter) and was placed in du Pont's Winterthur estate. *Courtesy of Annie A. Spring*

The work is not strictly mechanical. Artistic abilities are called upon, for in essence the rug hooker is painting with colorful rags. Large hand-hooked rugs are a project of the truly devoted; years of time and staggering amounts of material are required to complete the task.

Many room-sized hooked rugs are started with all the best intentions of being completed, but few ever reach the final stages. Huge half-finished patterns of carefully thought out rugs, accompanied by overflowing boxes of pre-cut wool, often become the inhabitants of a dusty attic.

Today sizeable hand hooked rugs are scarce. Though the craft of rug hooking is alive and well with strong numbers of active rug hookers, few individuals are able to devote such time and energy to hooking one rug. Those who have hooked a rug of grand proportion rarely sell their work. Only a very small number of professional rug makers will accept the overwhelming job of custom hooking a room size rug for a per square foot fee.

Large antique hooked rugs, those at least 100 years of age, are rare. Subjected to decades of daily foot traffic, a sizable hooked rug in need of repair was often cut down into one or several smaller rugs. Also older hooked rugs of large dimension deemed to be in poor condition were frequently discarded by owners unaware of the services of those who specialize in restoring antique hooked rugs.

A 1926 Antique Trading Post advertisment. Although he offered more than hooked rugs, his extensive inventory earned Ralph W. Burnham the title of "Hooked Rug Magnate." *Courtesy of Annie A. Spring*

Burnham's Antique Trading Post, Old Bay Road, Ipswich, Mass.

....1926

To M..

....

Dear..............................

Of 648 Old Hooked and Braided Rugs, sent to me by New England folks during the last six weeks, I bought 612; only 36 of that vast amount were returned. I call that good. It proved to me that folks were willing to send their Rugs to me to be priced, and that my offers for the Rugs pleased them. I hope to buy twice as many more during the next few weeks. Now, M...... ...., if you have Rugs to sell, or know of any that may be bought, write me fully about them; tell me how many you have, the sizes, colors and designs. I will then let you know if I wish you to send the Rugs to me, and I will send you shipping tags for that purpose. You will ask, "What do you pay for Rugs?" That I cannot tell until I see them and judge of their worth to me. The only way for me to see them is for you to send them to me. I will then write you my best offer. If you accept it, payment will be made at once. If you do not accept my offer, Rugs will be returned at my expense.

BIG MONEY PAID FOR LARGE-SIZE RUGS. In 1917 I paid Mr. T. A. Howe, Ipswich, Mass., $100. for a Rug 40 inches wide by 80 inches long. It is No. 152 on page 26 in my 44-Page Book on Hooked Rugs. I paid a lady in Dover, N. H., $600. for one Hooked Rug. I paid John A. Borrows, Portland, Maine, $1200. for one Hooked Rug. I paid $2600. to a man for a collection of 50 Hooked Rugs that he picked up in and around Waldoboro, Maine. These, of course, are unusual prices I paid for unusually artistic Rugs, but it goes to show what I will pay if the right Rugs are sent to me. If you sell a Hooked Rug to a person who knocks at your door the chances are that, sooner or later, it will reach me.

Burnham's is the place where they cash in on Hooked Rugs and Braided Rugs.

Hooked rugs purchased from Ralph W. Burnham decorate a Middleton, Massachusetts home built in 1680 by Captain Hook, thought to be the infamous high seas pirate. Photo from the 1920s. *Courtesy of Annie A. Spring*

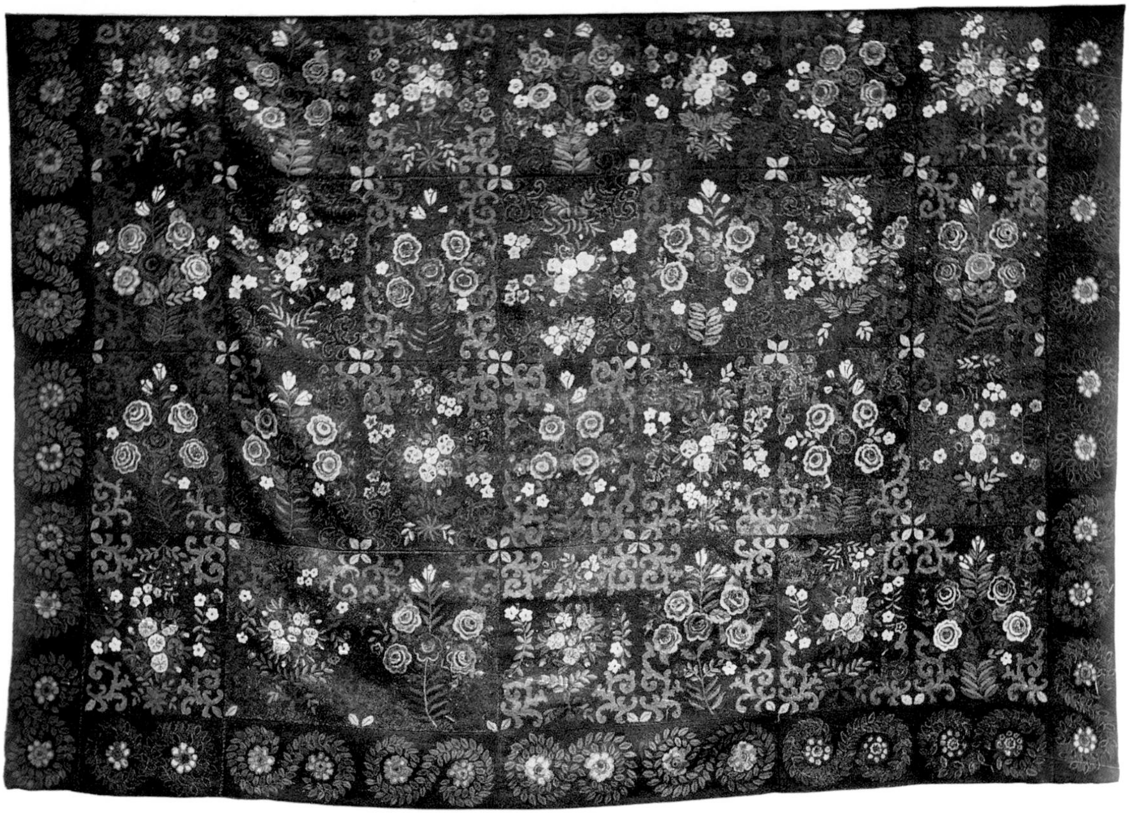

Due to its large dimensions, the entire surface of this floral hooked rug could not be properly photographed. Hung between three windows on the outside wall of a building, the rug is folded over a length of wooden strapping and we are unaware of its true proportions. The rug was hooked in sections and sewn together. From the Burnham Collection. Circa 1910. *Courtesy of Annie A. Spring*

A jungle of garden growth dwarfs the dainty scrolls of this elaborate hooked rug. From the Burnham Collection. Circa 1900. *Courtesy of Annie A. Spring*

A wonderful rug from the Burnham Collection. Hooked in South Berwick, Maine about 1879. In 1937, Burnham noted that this rug was purchased by a customer in New Jersey. 7′ x 9′. *Courtesy of Annie A. Spring*

Bouquets of leaves are bordered by more foliage and dainty flower. From the Burnham Collection. Circa 1900. *Courtesy of Annie A. Spring*

Large geometric hooked rugs of simple design were popular with Ralph Burnham's customers. From the Burnham Collection. Circa 1900. *Courtesy of Annie A. Spring*

An oval hooked rug of sizable dimension is the focal point of the room it graces. From the Burnham Collection. Circa 1910. *Courtesy of Annie A. Spring*

This rug of grand proportions was hooked with woolen yarns and sheared to give its surface a velvety sheen. Circa 1925. 13′ 2″ x 18′ 4″. *Collection of Alan Goldstein and Judith Taylor / Fine Arts, Fine Rugs*

Hooking this repetitious pattern must have been a tedious task for its maker. Dated 1954, the rug bears the initials DWA. 8′ 6″ x 11′ 6″.

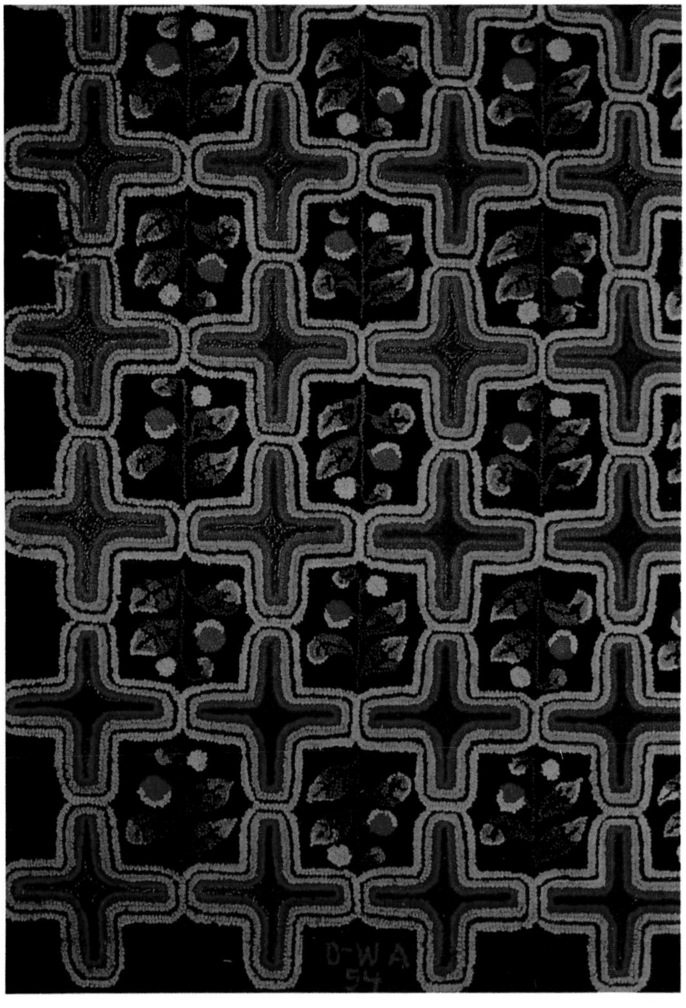

Detail shows the simple design hooked with a limited palette.

Harriett B. Claridge of New Hampshire works upon "Revival," a rug designed by Jane McGown Flynn. Finished size 7′ 6″ x 10′ 6″. *Photo by Joan Moshimer*

As she enjoys the Florida sun, Esther Jackson of Rhode Island works to complete her large hooked rug. Esther teaches and is a prominent member of the Association of Traditional Hooking Artists (ATHA). She has been responsible for promoting the joys of rug hooking through exhibits, demonstrations and newsletters. *Photo courtesy of Esther Jackson*

Susan Morin of Georgia hooks "Jericho," a Lib Calloway design. Finished size 6′ x 8′. *Photo courtesy of Susan Morin*

Marion N. Ham and "Fascination" the rug she designed and hooked are pictured outside her home in Brunswick, Maine. An accomplished designer and teacher, Marion offers rug hooking workshops that attract students from as far away as Brazil. 9′ x 12′. *Photo courtesy of Marion N. Ham*

"Fascination," designed and hooked by Marion N. Ham, captures the qualitites of a primitive painting. 9′ x 12′. *Photo courtesy of Marion N. Ham*

Amy N. Scott passed away before finishing this floral rug that she started to hook in the 1960s. Every color worked was dyed over white wool material. Finished size 7′ x 9′. *Courtesy of Phyllis S. Clukay. Photo by Susan L. Smidt*

Detail of carefully shaded hibiscus flowers and foliage.

Detail of the scroll that frames the hooked garden of flowers.

Detail of tulips, irises and other garden flowers.

The late Ethel Bruce, much beloved Massachusetts rug hooking teacher holds "Ethel's Endowment" a rug designed for her by Pearl K. McGown. Ethel was responsible for instructing hundreds of rug hooking students. She continued to teach, often traveling across the United States until her death at the age of 92.

"Round Phlox Floral," an Heirloom pattern hooked by Janet Bandilli won second prize at the 1992 Eastern Exposition in West Springfield, Massachusetts. Diameter 6′.

"Gainsboro," a Pearl K. McGown pattern, is being worked by Naomi Stopher, a rug hooking teacher from Georgia. Diameter 5″. *Photo courtesy of Naomi Stopher*

Detail of Janet Bandilli's "Round Phlox Floral"; a colorful hooked garden of flowers.

"Round Phlox Floral," an Heirloom pattern recently hooked by Myrna Mason of Tennessee. Diameter 6′. *Photo by Jeanne Edwards*

Mary Irma Worley recently hooked "Victorian Round," a Jane McGown Flynn pattern. Diameter 4′ 8″. *Photo by Jeanne Edwards*

"Istanbul," a Jane McGown Flynn pattern, hooked by Jane Curtin in 1988. Diameter 5′.

Detail of fanciful bird and foliage.

Susan L. Smidt hand-dyed the wool material used to hook "Lucetta's Tree of Life,"a Pearl K. McGown pattern. A scaffolding was required to hang the finished piece in the two story foyer where it is prominently displayed. Hooked in the 1980s. 5′ x 7′ 6″.

"Cumberland Crewel," a Joan Moshimer design, was hooked by Jane Curtin. The rug combines a border that imitates embroidered tapestry with an open field of mottled blues. 4′ 6″ x 6′.

"Victorian Square," a Pearl K. McGown pattern was hooked by Mildred Sacco in 1966. 7′ x 7′. *Photo courtesy of Mildred Sacco*

The pattern for this rug was purchased through an Alabama newspaper ad in 1952. Novice rug maker, Catherine Taff, cut all strips of wool by hand and hooked the large project with a tool crafted by her husband. 9′ x 12′. *Photo courtesy of Catherine Taff*

"Chinese Antiquity" a Pearl K. McGown pattern was hooked by Virginia Sheldon, a Massachusetts rug hooking teacher. She started work on the large rug in 1975 and completed her task in 1979. 8′ 4″ x 10′ 9″. *Photo courtesy of Virginia Sheldon*

Catherine Taff has nearly completed "Persian Palm," a Pearl K. McGown pattern. Her choice of soft colors is pleasing to the eye. 9′ x 12′. *Photo courtesy of Catherine Taff*

"Persian Palm," Pearl K. McGown's pattern, hooked by Mary Brandt Murphy in 1984. 6′ x 9′. *Photo courtesy of Mary Brandt Murphy*

Details reveal a harmonious balance of color. *Photo courtesy of Mary Brandt Murphy*

Mary Brandt Murphy chose to hook "Empress," a Pearl K. McGown pattern, in vivid colors. 4′ x 6′. *(Photo courtesy of Mary Brandt Murphy*

"Bergama," a New Earth Design pattern. By hooking her strips of dyed wool in a horizonatal direction, Elizabeth Rowe has recreated the appearance of a woven Oriental carpet. 4′ x 5′ 6″. *Photo courtesy of Elizabeth Rowe*

Martha Kendrick hooked a traditional quilt pattern for her son's home in Vermont. Woolen plaid materials were used to create this graphic area rug. 6′ x 9′. *Photo courtesy Martha Kendrick*

The shades of blue and white found in Canton china inspired New Hampshire rug hooking teacher, Hallie H. Hall, to hook this rug for her dining room. 7′ 8″ x 9′.

Rectangles, leaves and scrolls frame a field of hit or miss strips. Circa 1945. 8′ 5″ x 8′ 4″. *Private collection of S. Culler*

Detail shows the simplicity of the designs hooked in the border.

4 To Furnish a Home

Beauport

Henry Davis Sleeper (1878-1934) built his 40 room summer cottage **Beauport** on the shores of the Atlantic Ocean in Gloucester, Massachusetts. As a well known interior designer, Mr. Sleeper utilized his talents to decorate the estates of an elite clientele, including the du Pont and Vanderbilt families. His passion for collecting filled Beauport with an eccentric array of antique furniture, period accessories and large number of hooked rugs. After Sleeper's death in 1934, the house and it contents were purchased by the McCann family, heirs to the F. W. Woolworth fortune. Though pursued by collectors and museum curators to sell Sleeper's possessions, the McCann children, following the wishes of their deceased parents, presented Beauport in its entirety to The Society for the Preservation of New England Antiquities.

The Beauport-Sleeper, McCann House, summer retreat of interior designer Henry Davis Sleeper, is located along the shore of the Atlantic Ocean in Gloucester, Massachusetts. The property, now owned by The Society for the Preservation of New England Antiquities, is open to the public from May through October.

The Beauport-Sleeper McCann House is open to the public from May 15 through October 15. On view in the museum is a partial inventory of Mr. Sleeper's hooked rugs, as seen in *Hooked Rugs: History and the Continuing Tradition*. With the permission of The Society for the Preservation of New England Antiquities and assistance of Beauport's site administrator Barbara Tarr, I was able to photograph the larger hooked rugs that Mr. Sleeper owned. Due to age and deterioration from years of foot traffic the hooked rugs pictured are no longer on display.

A variety of textiles were utilized to create the many flowers hooked in the rug appropriately named "Garden by the Sea." Circa 1880. *Property of S.P.N.E.A.*

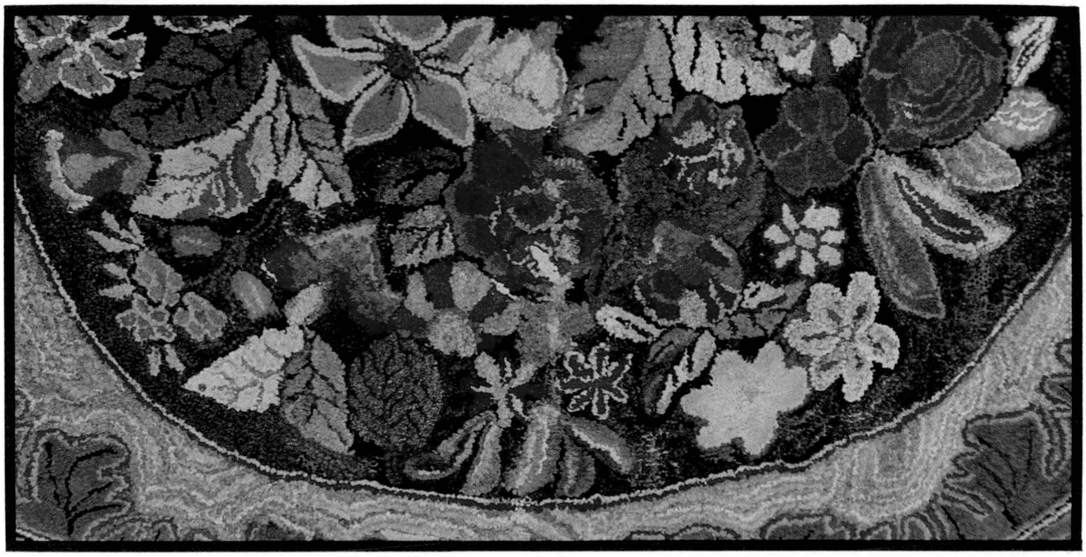

Detail of the center portion of "Garden by the Sea." The large rug was hooked in two sections and then sewn together as indicated by the seam that runs through the floral design. *Property of S.P.N.E.A.*

Hooked from woolen yarns, this rug of classic design once graced Mr. Sleeper's music room. Circa 1910. 6′ x 8′. *Property of S.P.N.E.A.*

A central bouquet of carnation-like flowers is encircled by S-shaped scroll links. Floral spandrels border the rug. Circa 1880. 6′ 8″ x 7′ 2″. *Property of S.P.N.E.A.*

Detail of carnation-like flower and S-shaped link scroll.

Alternating roses and harp-shaped designs surround a colorful medallion of flowers. Circa 1900. 6′ 1″ x 7′ 7″. *Property of S.P.N.E.A.*

Maple leaf runner, possibly of Canadian origins. Hooked of woolen yarn. Originally used on Beauport's main staircase. Circa 1910. 1′ 6″ x 21′ 6″. *Property of S.P.N.E.A.*

Detail shows wear on the tread and good condition of the riser.

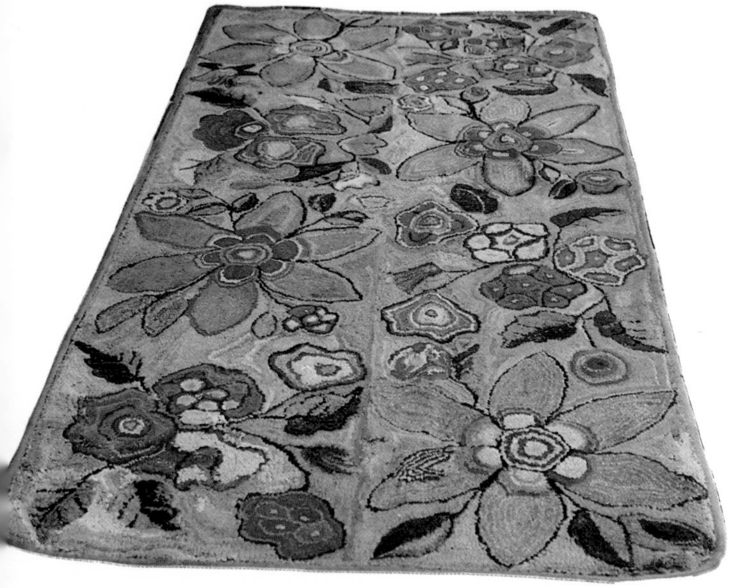

Bold, imaginative flowers were hooked on a neutral ground. Circa 1900. 3′ 4″ x 7′ 4″. *Property of S.P.N.E.A.*

Conkey

Helen Conkey's daughter was reluctant to sell the 6′ x 9′ hooked rug her mother had made for the newlyweds' first apartment. But Helen did have an interested buyer and promised Dorothea she would hook her "something better" if the four year old gift was relinquished. The rug was sold.

"Something better" arrived six years later in the form of an enlarged version of the rug Dorothea had parted with. The room size, 12′ x 18′ hooked rug was a pattern of autumn oak leaves and acorns fashioned from worn family clothing and wool rags. Certain areas of blue were hooked from the Navy uniform that Helen's husband wore during World War I.

Helen Conkey began hooking rugs in 1941. She felt it made sense to be able to create something practical yet pleasing to the eye from materials that ordinarily would have been discarded. Throughout New England, Helen became a sought after instructor and speaker. She spent four summers teaching rug hooking and design concepts at the University of Tennessee. Helen Conkey continued to craft rugs and inspire others well past her eightieth birthday.

My son, Rob, sits at the far end of the 12′ x 18′ rug hooked by Helen Conkey. After six years of labor, the rug was completed in 1962.

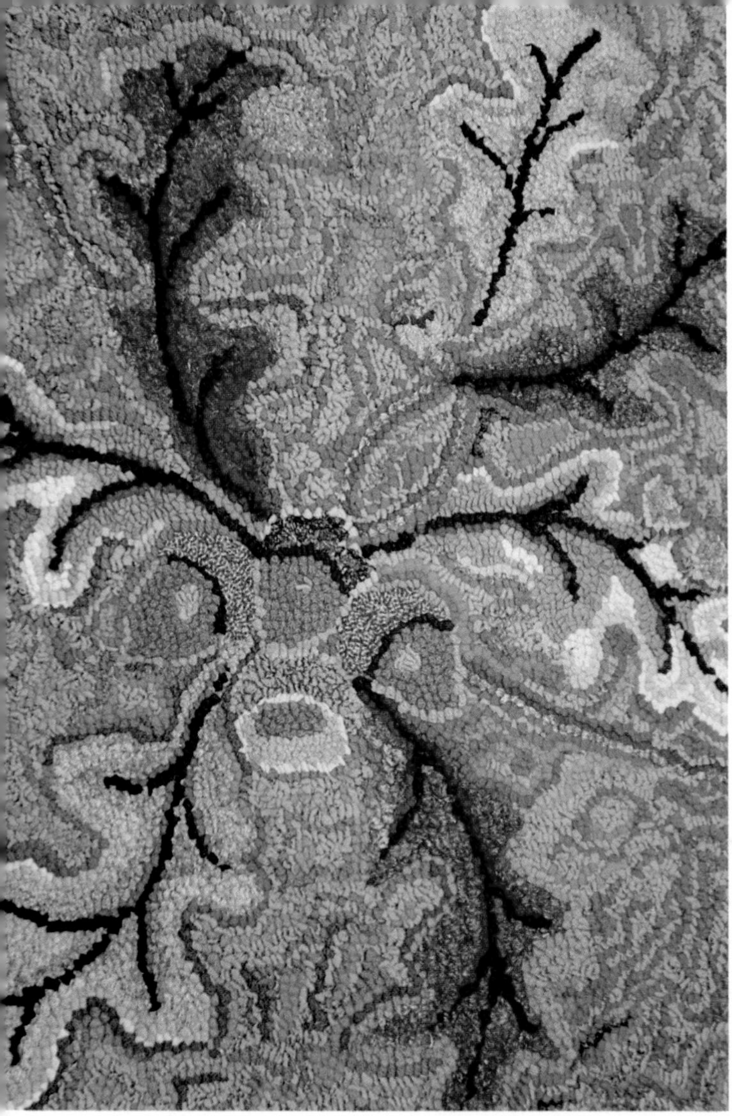

Detail of the rug's field shows the many shades of blue used. Helen Conkey preferred to hook with as is materials; recycling old woolen clothing worn by family members.

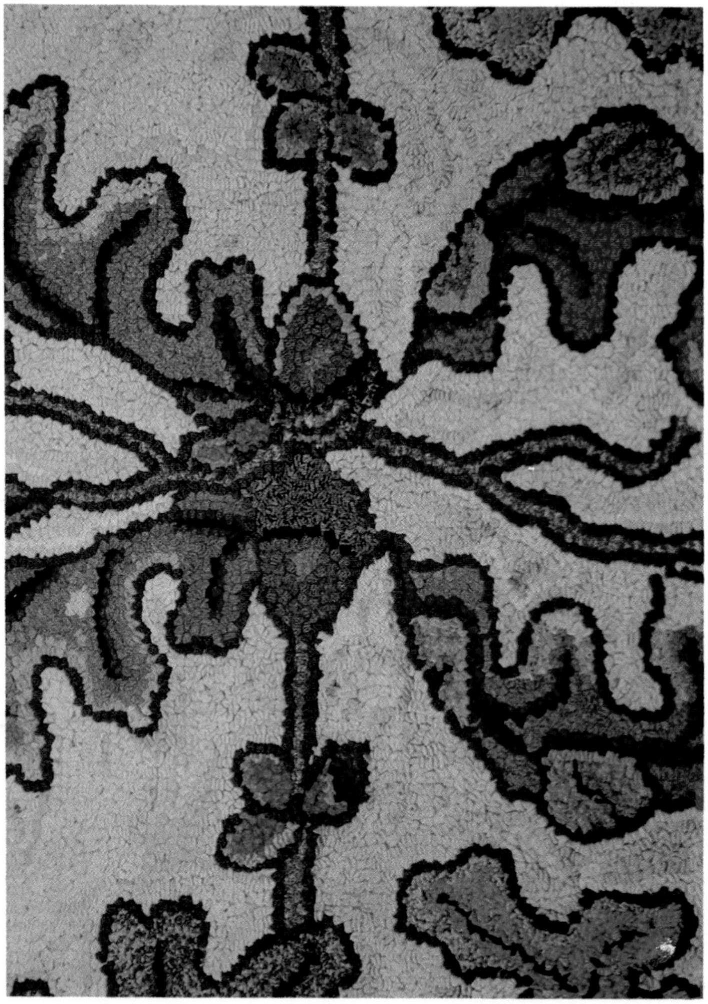

Detail illustrates how a change of background color can effect the subject hooked.

Detail of the border. Helen Conkey hooked her name and those of other family members into the border of the rug.

Detail of the rug's edge and partial blue field.

Martin House/Colonial Dames

The Martin Farm House was built in the early 1700's in the small township of Swansea, Massachusetts. Originally constructed as a one room dwelling, additions were made over the years to meet the needs of its occupants. The farm house, two barns, and 38 acres of field and woodlands remained in the Martin family for over 200 years. In 1935 the property was willed to the National Society of the Colonial Dames in the Commonwealth of Massachusetts by the bequest of Mrs. Susan Taber Martin Allien, an eighth generation Martin. Placed on the National Register of Historic Properties in 1979, the Martin House is a rare example of an 18th and early 19th century New England farm. The Dames open the museum house to the public from May 1 to November 1, Wednesday through Saturday and Sunday afternoons.

The house is furnished with Colonial and Federal period antiques, including a unique collection of 17th century English Jacobean furniture. Of special interest are the half-tester bedstead and three flat tester bedsteads [circa 1750-1820] dressed in documented bed hangings made of reproduction fabrics and hand sewn by members of the Colonial Dames. Early pewter, samplers and hooked rugs are also on display.

Located in Swansea, Massachusetts, Martin House is a rare example of an 18th to early 19th century New England farm.

Popular Frost pattern of a horse with simple leaf designs. Late nineteenth century. *Property of the Martin House Farm*

Design of hearts and geometric shapes makes a simple but charming rug. Early twentieth century. *Property of the Martin House Farm*

A slightly askew basket of flowers with abundant foliage is framed by a bold border. Hooked from a printed pattern. Late nineteenth century. *Property of the Martin House Farm*

Wide-eyed spaniel hooked from a Frost pattern is draped over a painted trunk. Late nineteenth century. *Property of the Martin House Farm*

Though it retains elements similar to a rug hooked from a printed pattern, the simple floral motif has child-like qualities. Early twentieth century. *Property of the Martin House Farm*

5 The Mills-Mosseller Studio

When studying hooked rugs of grand proportion and those that embellish grand places, one would be amiss not to make note of the hand crafted carpets made at the Mills-Mosseller Studio in Tryon, North Carolina. Mills-Mosseller rugs have graced the Governor's mansions in Richmond, Virginia and in Raleigh, North Carolina; Roosevelt's Little White House in Warm Springs, Georgia; The Smithsonian Institution in Washinton, D.C.; and a baron's estate in Belgium. Only four or five large custom-designed hooked rugs are produced in this studio per year.

The Mills-Mosseller rugs come to life by means of a wooden shuttle hook, cousin to the traditional tool favored by other hooking artists. Origins of shuttle hooking can be traced to the mid-1800's. The operating mechanics of this hand held tool and that of the sewing machine are similar. Long strips of fabric or lengths of wool or cotton yarn are fed through the eye of the hook. By poking the eye through a design printed on the underside of a woven foundation and sliding the shuttle back and forth, a loop is formed on the opposite side of the pattern. The back of the piece faces the shuttle hooker as he or she creates the thousands of uniform loops that will compose the top surface of the finished carpet. It takes two and a half hours to hook a square foot of plain background. Complicated patterns with many small details and several changes of color require more time.

Lillian Mills Mosseller's first job was painting delicate designs on furniture for a decorator in Asheville, North Carolina during 1925. Each week a woman from the Carolina Mountains would sell the shop owner a hooked rug; always the same pattern of roses fashioned from garish colors. When Mrs. Mosseller inquired as to why she did not use a different design and dye some pleasing colors to hook with, the woman informed her that she owned only one printed pattern and knew nothing about dyes.

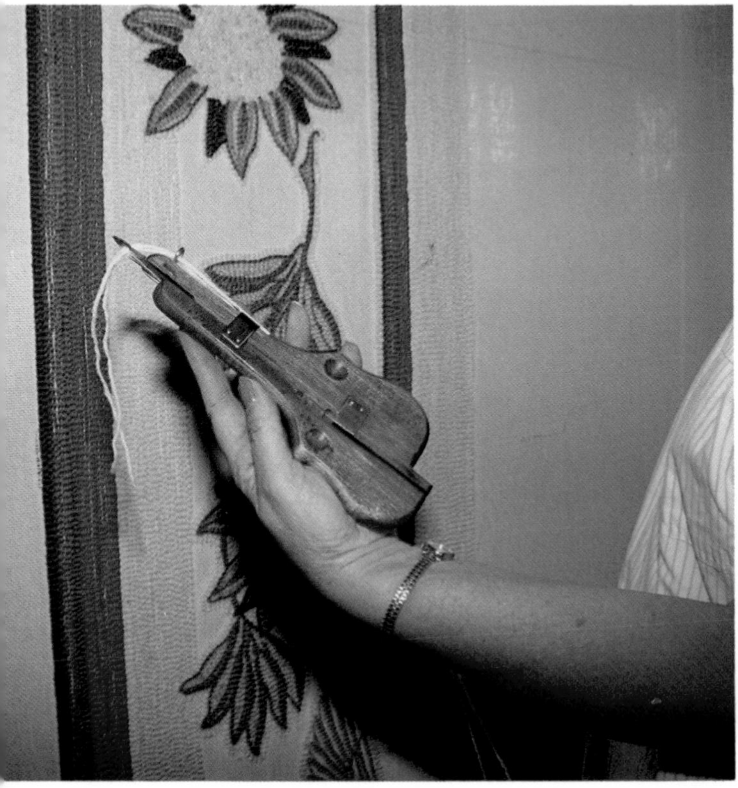

The operating mechanics of a wooden shuttle hook are similar to those of a sewing machine. Woolen yarns are fed through the eye of the hook.

A pattern is printed on sturdy, woven cotton. The eye of the hook is poked through the design. By moving the shuttle back and forth loops are formed on the opposite side of the pattern,

When Lillian Mills-Mosseller made an offer to draw new motifs and do some experimenting with tinting woolen yarns, she was launched into a new career. With a staff of North Carolina craftspeople she moved to New York and became established as a supplier of artistic hooked carpeting. Between 1916 and 1933 the demand for hand-hooked rugs was far greater than the supply. In 1916, B. Altman in New York City featured a display of antique hooked rugs in their store windows.

The response to the handsome, old handcrafted rugs was overwhelming, but the numbers of available rugs for sale was limited. To fill the demand, cottage industries formed in New England and the Carolinas with rug hookers working overtime to furnish the hand crafted carpets sought by anxious interior decorators. The New York City studio attracted an impressive clientele; Mills-Mosseller hooked rugs were and continue to be a decorating asset in the most prestigious homes and public buildings across the United States.

After World War II, Mrs. Mosseller moved the studio back to North Carolina and continued to offer artistic hooked carpeting to selected buyers. Her son Ronald, who is responsible for designing many of the important rugs in the Mills-Mosseller collection, maintains the business his mother founded. Attention to quality and the ability to produce exquisite hooked works of art have earned the Mills-Mosselller Studio of Tryon, North Carolina an enviable reputation.

A rug worker hooks in the background of a large custom-designed rug.

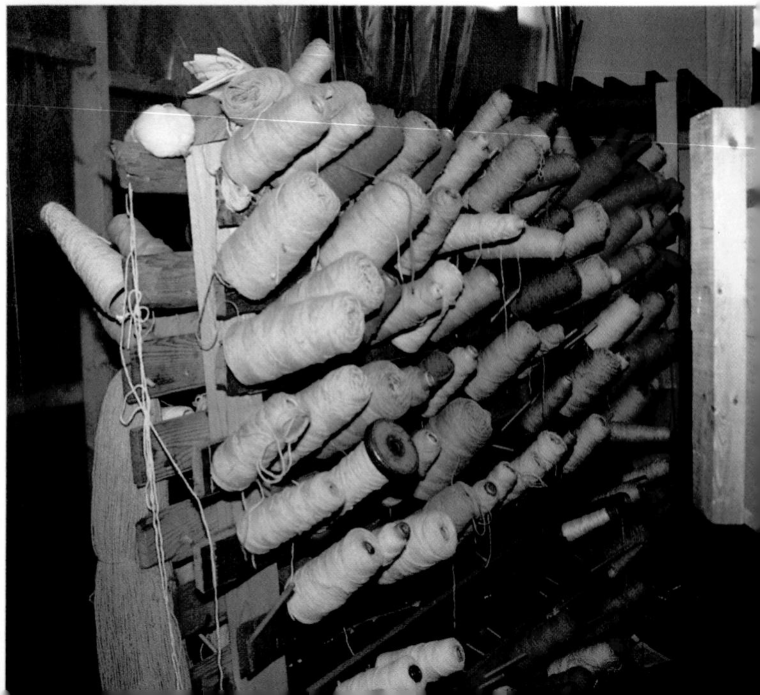

The yarns used at the Mills-Mosseller Studio are one hundred per cent wool. All dyeing is done on the premises. The cones of wool pictured represent only a small portion of what will be needed to complete a rug.

Once the design is printed upon a cotton foundation, the pattern is stretched on a wooden frame that stands upright in the studio. Due to their large size, the shuttle worker must use scaffolding to reach upper portions of the rug.

When the shuttle hooking process is completed, the surface of the rug is sheared. Shearing off the tops of the woolen loops gives the rug a velvety sheen. "Regency George IV" designed by Romne (trade name used by Ronald Mosseller) was made at the Mills-Mosseller Studio for the Williamsburg Inn, Williamsburg, Virginia. The finished rug was placed in the ballroom. *Photo courtesy of The Mills-Mosseller Studio*

During the 1960s, the Smithsonian Institution in Washington D.C., commissioned the Mills-Mosseller Studio to design and hook three rugs for the First Ladies' Hall. Pictured is the Grant Room rug. The Romne design was inspired by a fragment of carpet shown in an old photograph of the White House Blue Room during the Grant Administration. Many months were spent hooking the 10′ x 14′ oval, with one worker taking three months just to hook the tiny rose buds. *Photo courtesy of The Mills-Mosseller Studio*

" The 19th Day" by Romne. *Photo courtesy of The Mills-Mosseller Studio*

"Regency #3" was designed by Romne for a Williamsburg Inn suite. *Photo courtesy of The Mills-Mosseller Studio*

A client in Chicago commissioned "Regency Hall,"a design by Romne. At the time the photograph was taken the shearing process was unfinished. *Photo courtesy of The Mills-Mosseller Studio*

"The Four Muses" by Romne. *Photo courtesy of The Mills-Mosseller Studio*

"Ming Dynasty Mountain Top" by Romne. *Photo courtesy of The Mills-Mosseller Studio*

Unfinished "Regency-Empire" showing the underside of the rug. Designed by Romne. *Photo courtesy of The Mills-Mosseller Studio*

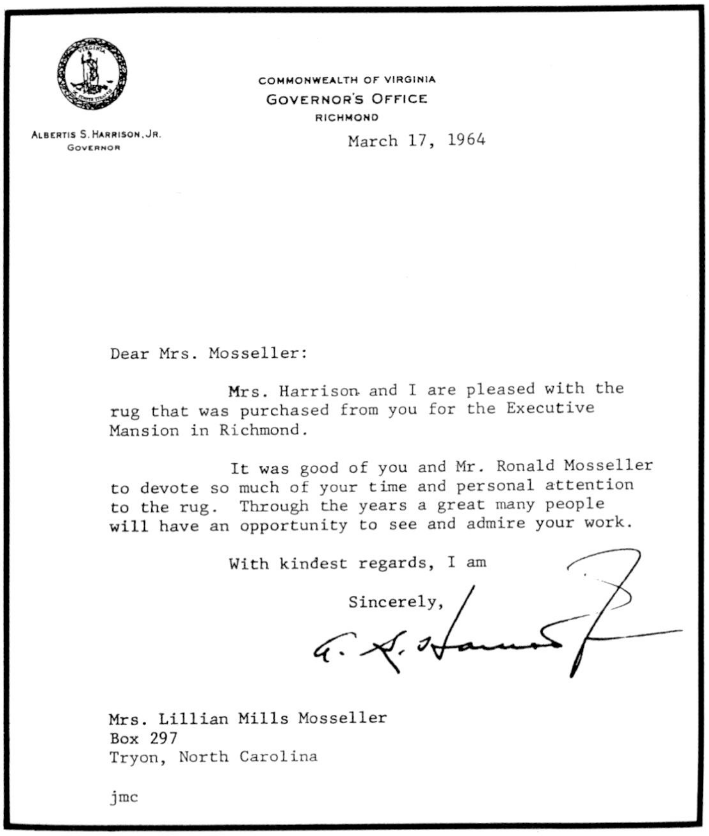

COMMONWEALTH OF VIRGINIA
GOVERNOR'S OFFICE
RICHMOND

ALBERTIS S. HARRISON, JR.
GOVERNOR

March 17, 1964

Dear Mrs. Mosseller:

Mrs. Harrison and I are pleased with the rug that was purchased from you for the Executive Mansion in Richmond.

It was good of you and Mr. Ronald Mosseller to devote so much of your time and personal attention to the rug. Through the years a great many people will have an opportunity to see and admire your work.

With kindest regards, I am

Sincerely,

Mrs. Lillian Mills Mosseller
Box 297
Tryon, North Carolina

jmc

Complimentary letter dated March 17, 1964, from Governor Albertis S. Harrison Jr. of Virginia.

"Coffee and Cream" designed by Lillian M. Mosseller was exhibited at the Metropolitan Museum of Art in New York City during 1937. The International Exhibit of Rugs and Carpets featured 116 pieces represented by thirteen countries. The embossed hooked rug whose design was inspired by Mrs. Mosseller's morning cup of coffee was the only American-made rug in the show. 9′ x 9′. *Photo courtesy of The Mills-Mosseller Studio*

The Lincoln Room rug in the First Ladies' Hall was designed by Lillian M. Mosseller. After an extensive and fruitless search for examples of carpeting used in the White House during the Lincoln Administration, it was decided that a Victorian period motif would coordinate well with the wallpaper and room furnishings. Approximate size 20′ x 21′. *Photo courtesy of The Mills-Mosseller Studio*

An oval within an exterior polygon, the dining room was designed by a Richmond architect, Duncan Lee. Following its contours, the hand-loomed rug repeats the design of the frieze in the upstairs hall and on the ballroom mantles. William Byrd, II, founder of Richmond, presides in oil.

Over three hundred shades of blue and green were hand dyed one skein at a time by Ronald Mosseller for the rug that was placed in the Virginia Executive Mansion dining room for governor Albertis S. Harrison during the 1960s. The 18′ x 30′ oval, designed by Romne, repeats architectural elements found throughout the Richmond estate. *Photo courtesy of The Mills-Mosseller Studio*

6 Grand People and Places

Crafted from worn clothing, discarded rags and burlap, hand-hooked rugs brought warmth and touches of color to modest homes during the latter half of the nineteenth century. Yet humble origins did not confine hooked rugs to simple dwellings. As the popularity of the craft grew and their appeal became apparent to the non-hooking public, the once humble hooked rug traveled uptown to cushion the footsteps of the rich and famous.

Hooked rugs have graced the floors of The Vatican, The White House and manors of European nobility. The du Ponts of Winterthur followed the advice of interior designer Henry Sleeper and collected the rag and wool beauties for their estate. Texas heiress Ima Hogg had her chaffeur drive to New England to visit Ralph Burnham, "Hooked Rug Magnate" of Ipswich, Massachusetts, for the sole purpose of purchasing hooked rugs. In his book *Bette & Joan: The Divine Feud*, author Shaun Considine describes an at-home scene of screen starlet Joan Crawford and her soon to be husband, Franchot Tone. Before a blazing fire, Tone would read aloud the words of great writers as Joan listened and worked upon her hooked rugs.

From the turn of the century to present day, hooked rugs have held a small but important niche of the interior decorating world. The story is truly one of rags to riches.

The home-arts craze that swept across the country during the 1930s did not leave Hollywood untouched. Actress Joan Crawford takes time from a busy movie making schedule to relax and work on her rug. In addition to hooking rugs Miss Crawford was often seen knitting on the sets of her pictures. *Photo from the early 1930s*

In 1946, Massachusetts rug hooking mentor Pearl K. McGown sent her sister Kaddy to open a West Coast store and offer lessons to anxious students. The rug-filled windows of the Sherman Oaks, California shop attracted many visitors. Actor Clark Gable frequently passed by and stopped to admire the hooked handiwork.

Actress Shirley Booth decorated her Cape Cod, Massachusetts summer home with hooked rugs.

Ingrid McBrian, from Shelter Island, New York, took two long trips around the world. As a tribute to the countries visited, she designed and hooked "One World." The 9′ 5″ x 15′ 3″ rug was made during the 1950s and was exhibited in many places and received several awards, including a blue ribbon at the Women's International Exposition in New York City. Grey cloud-like shapes surround the center hemispheres. The pyramids of Egypt, Great Wall of China, pyramids of Yucatan and the Cliff Dwellers; each of these four wonders occupies a corner of the rug.

Eighteen hooked replicas of well-known landmarks are encircled by a rope border. She included the following scenes from her journeys: (1) The United Nations in New York, USA; (2) Lake Louise in Alberta, Canada; (3) Grand Canyon in Arizona, USA; (4) The 18th Century Cathedral in Taxco, Mexico; (5) The Citadel built by Henri Christophe in Haiti; (6) Mount of Fire above rice fields of Indonesia; (7) Mosque in Northern Nigeria; (8) The Campanile in Port Elizabeth, South Africa; (9) A view of Sydney, Australia from the bridge that spans the harbor; (10) European office of the United Nations in Geneva, Switzerland; (11) Cathedral of St. Basil in Moscow, Russia; (12) Eiffel Tower in Paris, France; (13) the Taj Mahal in India; (14) Fuji, Sacred Mount of Japan; (15) Machu Picchu, Sanctuary of the Virgins of the Sun, Peru; (16) La Paz, founded in 1548 in Bolivia; (17) Gauchos herding cattle in Argentina; (18) Christ the Redeemer crowning Corovado in Rio de Janeiro, Brazil. *Photo courtesy of Sandy Vohr.*

Royal Treatment

In 1939, Their Majesties King George VI and Queen Elizabeth made a tour of Canada and her Maritime Provinces. On July 14, the Royal Yacht arrived at Prince Edward Island and was secured at the Charlottetown wharf. The Lieutenant-Governor, The Honorable George DeBlois and his entire entourage welcomed the Royal Couple as they came ashore. Their stay on the island lasted but a few hours. Despite its brevity, the Royal Visit was deemed a smashing success.

The maker of the rug pictured is unknown. Perhaps it was hooked by a member of the cheering crowd that gathered to greet the King and Queen of England that day.

King George VI and Queen Elizabeth as they appeared aboard the Royal Train during the 1939 visit to Canada. *Photo courtesy of The Honorable Tom McMillan and Prince Edward Island Museum and Heritage Foundation, Prince Edward Island Public Archives and Records Office*

King George VI left his yacht and came ashore on the Charlottetown wharf, July 14, 1939. *Photo courtesy of The Honorable Tom McMillan and Prince Edward Island Public Archives and Record Office*

Perhaps the maker of this rug was part of the cheering crowd that came to greet the King and Queen of England. Hooked of woolen yarns. 27″ x 44″. *Courtesy of The Honorable Tom McMillan*

FDR

In the summer of 1921 a young New York lawyer with political aspirations was stricken by poliomyelitis. The dreaded virus left Franklin Delano Roosevelt paralyzed from the waist down. After three years of all the treatment and cures his prominent family's wealth could buy, there was little evidence of any improvement in his weaken muscles or depressed spirit.

Through word of another polio patient, Roosevelt learned of a small community 80 miles southwest of Atlanta with naturally warmed pure mineral waters. The buoyancy of the water combined with a consistent 88 degree temperature soothed weakened muscles and made strength regaining exercises possible without excessive fatigue. Franklin and his wife Eleanor traveled to the rural town of Bullockville, later to be renamed Warm Springs. Though the mineral waters could not reverse the damage caused by the polio virus, Roosevelt could comfortably swim for two hours.

This new found mobility boosted his spirits tremendously. Roosevelt encouraged others with polio to visit the therapeutic pools and began to vigorously pursue the political career that until this point he and all others had felt was over.

Roosevelt was elected governor of New York in 1928 and was re-elected in 1930. In the midst of the Great Depression, FDR was nominated for the Presidency by the Democratic party and won the 1932 race by a landslide. The United States was economically devastated by hundreds of bank closings and alarming numbers of unemployed men and women. Roosevelt brought to office the idea of turning government around. His New Deal philosophy was responsible for putting the country back on its feet, earning FDR the admiration of the American people.

President Franklin D. Roosevelt's Little White House in Warm Springs, Georgia. *Photo courtesy of the Georgia Department of Natural Resources, Parks and Historic Sites Division*

Roosevelt was elected to the Presidential office for four consecutive terms despite his disability. The public was unaware that the Commander-in-chief who had guided the United States through World War II was not able to walk or stand without assistance.

Warm Springs became a mecca for those who had suffered from the debilitating effects of polio. Through FDR's endorsements, a rehabilitation center, clinics and additional warm spring pools were constructed. Doctors and orthopedic specialists offered hope to the seemingly endless number of patients.

During his years as governor, FDR made frequent trips to the mineral water spa in Georgia. He went so far as to purchase a parcel of wooded land at the base of Pine Mountain near to the famous springs and build a small single-story cottage. Throughout his years in Washington, Franklin and Eleanor found peace and solitude in what was to be dubbed "The Little White House". Here during the afternoon of April 12, 1945, while reading his mail as his portrait was being painted, Roosevelt collapsed and died.

The Little White House is now a museum operated by the Georgia Department of Natural Resources, Parks and Historic Sites. The Warm Spring's cottage remains as it was when the Roosevelts were in residence. The President and First Lady chose to decorate their retreat with personal mementos, comfortable furniture and hooked rugs.

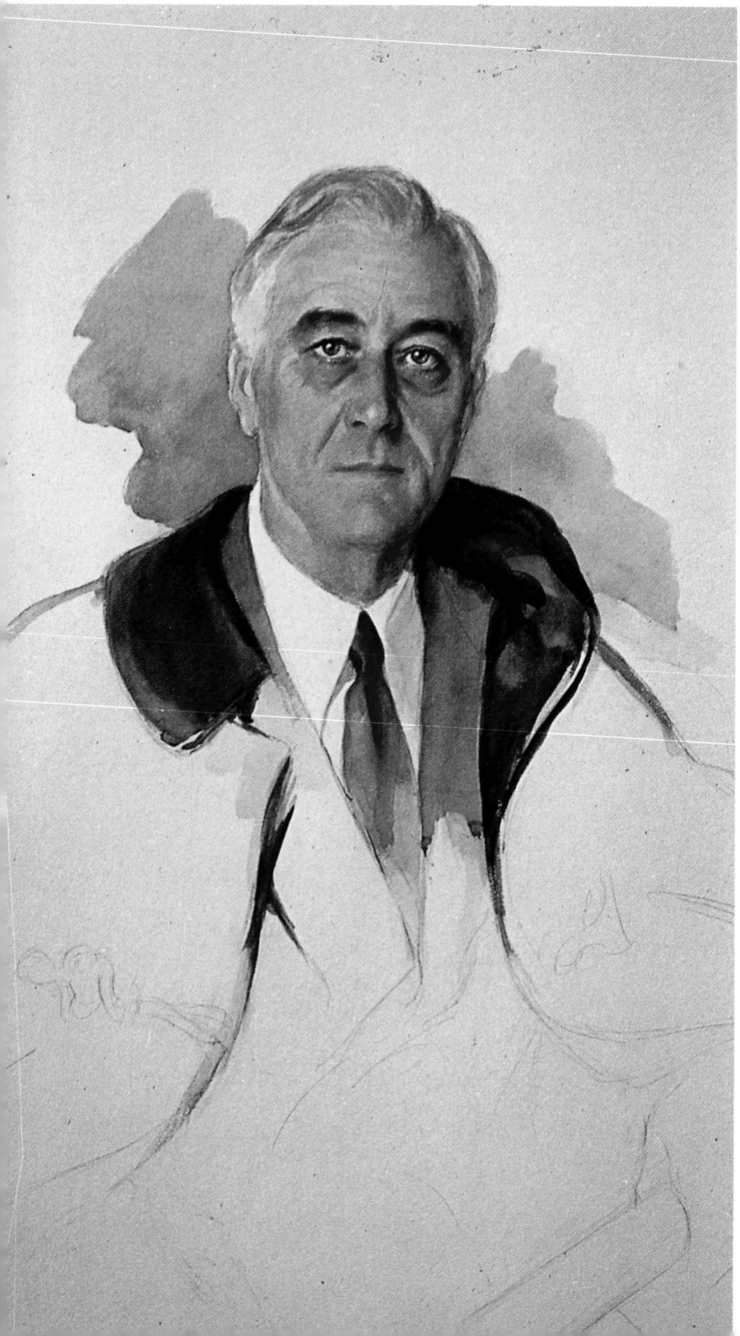

President Roosevelt was sitting for artist Elizabeth Shoumatoff when he suffered a fatal stroke on April 12, 1945. The famous unfinished portrait is displayed in the Little White House. *Photo courtesy of the Georgia Department of Natural Resources, Parks and Historic Sites Division*

Pictured is the living room area of Roosevelt's Little White House. The President was seated in this chair, reviewing his mail and having his portrait painted, when he collapsed and died. At his feet was the "New Deal" hooked rag rug, 7′ 10″ x 10′ x 10." Given to Roosevelt in 1933 by an anonymous donor, the words N-E-W D-E-A-L and NRA US appear on the rug along with symbols of his campaign: a small horse, seven horns of plenty and two blue eagles. The initials LM are worked into rug's floral, foliage and scroll motif; this is the mark of the rug's designer and maker who remained unknown until 1952. Lillian Mosseller of North Carolina was in Atlanta during 1952 discussing plans for a rug she had been commissioned to hook for a home in South Georgia. By chance she glanced upon the desk of the gentleman she was visiting and saw a newspaper article about Roosevelt's Little White House in Warm Springs. Pictured was the New Deal hooked rug. "Oh, for heaven's sake! I made that rug," she exclaimed. Nineteen years before the rug had been ordered by a decorator for a customer who insisted on anonymity. Mrs. Mosseller delivered the finished hooked rug to the decorator unaware of its future owner. This photo was taken 45 years ago when the site was being prepared for opening to the public. *Photo courtesy of the Georgia Department of Natural Resources, Parks and Historic Sites Division*

The New Deal rug as it appears today. *Courtesy of the Georgia Department of Natural Resources, Parks and Historic Sites Division*

The center medallion features a small horse surrounded by seven horns of plenty. The horse was a gift to President Roosevelt; the horns of plenty symbolizes prosperous times ahead. *Courtesy of the Georgia Department of Natural Resources, Parks and Historic Sites Division*

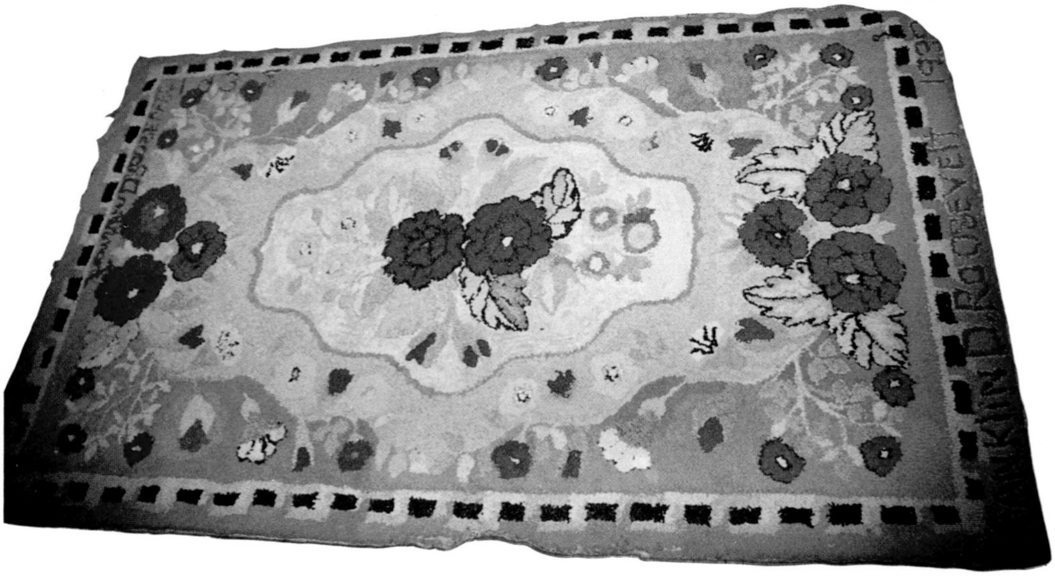

This brightly colored, scatter-size yarn hooked rug decorates the Little White House bedroom of President Roosevelt. *Courtesy of the Georgia Department of Natural Resources, Parks and Historic Sites Division*

Detail of one end of the rug showing the President's name hooked in block letters. *Courtesy of the Georgia Department of Natural Resources, Parks and Historic Sites Division*

Detail of the opposite end shows the President's name hooked in a combination of script and block letters.

One room in the Little White House functions as a combination living and dining area. Opposite the New Deal rug, a hooked rug of geometric pattern cushions the Roosevelt table and chairs. *Courtesy of the Georgia Department of Natural Resources, Parks and Historic Sties Division*

Salma S. Dhanji

North America is a melting pot of diverse cultures, colors and religions. The rug hooking community is no different. Ethnic backgrounds of women and men rug hookers are as widely varied as the rugs they work.

In 1975 Shiraz and Salma Dhanji and two sons left their native land of Bombay, India and traveled to the United States in search of better economic opportunities. The 10,000 mile journey brought the Moslem family to Pittsburgh, Pennsylvania. Shiraz pursued his career as an electronics engineer. Salma cared for her husband and children but found time to attend a rug hooking class at the YWCA. She faithfully studied the craft for four years.

By 1980 the Dhanjis had moved to Florida. In Fort Lauderdale, Salma offered rug hooking lessons. Skillfully she instructed her growing number of students in an art form indigenous to North America. Though accomplished in its many styles, Salma marries the technique of American rug hooking with Indian colors and designs. The combination is appealing.

In the United States, Salma was able to pursue her own business, a cherished freedom after the restraints of life in India. In appreciation for being so warmly accepted into the American community and having the chance to fulfill her dreams, Salma presented a sample of her rug hooking talents to the American people. The gift, an exquisitely worked replica of the Presidential seal, was personally delivered in February of 1985 to President Ronald Reagan at a White House meeting arranged by United States Representative E. Clay Shaw, Jr. The hooked seal took approximately seven months of work, laboring seven days a week for eight to ten hours per day. Each of the estimated 873,000 wool loops that make up the hooked rug were fashioned by Salma's hand.

The determined and charming woman from India is no longer a stranger in a foreign land. Her ability to master an American craft combined with excellent teaching skills have earned Salma many friends and a reputation as a respected rug hooking artist. Salma S. Dhanji continues to teach in Fort Lauderdale. Most recently she has offered to the public a catalog of her unique designs.

Rug hooking artist Salma S. Dhanji presents President Ronald Reagan with her gift to the American people; a hooked Presidential seal. Also pictured are her husband Shiraz and United States Representative E. Clay Shaw Jr., who was responsible for arranging the February, 1985 meeting. The 60" diameter seal took approximately seven months of work, seven days per week for eight to ten hours a day. Note that the stars were carefully shaded giving each a three dimensional look. *Photo courtesy of Salma S. Dhanji*

An Indian painting of the last Mughal Emperor Bhadur Shah II with two sons and an attendant, dated 1838, inspired Salma to hook this wall hanging. *Photo courtesy of Salma S. Dhanji*

"From Here to Eternity," designed and hooked by Salma S. Dhanji, was inspired by the artist's pilgrimage to Mecca in 1985. The center portion of the rug depicts stages in life on earth: newborn child, musician, philospher, virgin, cup bearer, master and slave, married couple and an aged man. Also present are the sun and moon, bird, fish and animals of the land. On the floral borders are angels with quill and scroll who record every detail and happening of man on earth. Superimposed in the top of the border is an Arabic verse from the Holy Quran. Translated, it reads, "Which of the Bounties of the Lord will ye deny." The verses on bottom left and right read, "The Lord of the East and the West" and "The Lord of the Heavens and the Earth." *Photo courtesy of Salma S. Dhanji*

"Indian Courtesan," a minature painting dating from the late 1600s, was enlarged and hooked by Salma in 1988. 24″ x 29″. *Photo courtesy of Salma S. Dhanji*

Salma designed and hooked a bright bouquet of roses, buds and foliage. The colors she worked were hand dyed. 40″ x 54″. *Photo courtesy of Salma S. Dhanji*

"Sunflowers" a pattern by Jane McGown Flynn, was hooked by Salma in 1990. 30" x 50". *Photo courtesy of Salma S. Dhanji*

A very unusual palette of color—pinks, purples, golds and turquoise—was chosen by Salma for this Turkish prayer rug. Pattern by Yankee Peddler. 36" x 54". *Photo courtesy of Salma S. Dhanji*

"Gulistan" designed and hooked by Salma. 48" x 72". *Photo courtesy of Salma S. Dhanji*

Detail of "Jacobean Fantasy," a Yankee Peddler pattern hooked by Salma. *Photo courtesy of Salma S. Dhanji*

Salma instructs her students during one of the classes she offers in Fort Lauderdale, Florida. *Photo courtesy of Salma S. Dhanji*

"Rosemarie's Shell Collection" designed by Salma and hooked by Rosemarie Martell. 27″ x 42″. *Photo courtesy of Salma S. Dhanji*

An Indian painting of Rajput Nobility was enlarged by Salma and hooked by Chiz Gilbert. 24" x 35". *Photo courtesy of Salma S. Dhanji*

"Indian Village Girl" was enlarged from a greeting card. The design was reproduced by Salma and hooked by Chiz Gilbert. The vivid colors are typical of Indian culture. 22" x 30". *Photo courtesy of Salma S. Dhanji*

Mary E. Philbrick made the Great Seal as a gift to Vice-President George Bush and his wife, Barbara. The occasion was a house-warming party the Bushes gave for families of the men who had repaired their Walker's Point, Kennebunkport, Maine home after it was damaged by severe storm waves in 1981. Pictured from right to left are Longley Philbrick, George Bush, Mary L. Philbrick, hooked rug artist Mary E. Philbrick, Barbara Bush and Wally Davis. *Photo courtesy of Mary E. Philbrick*

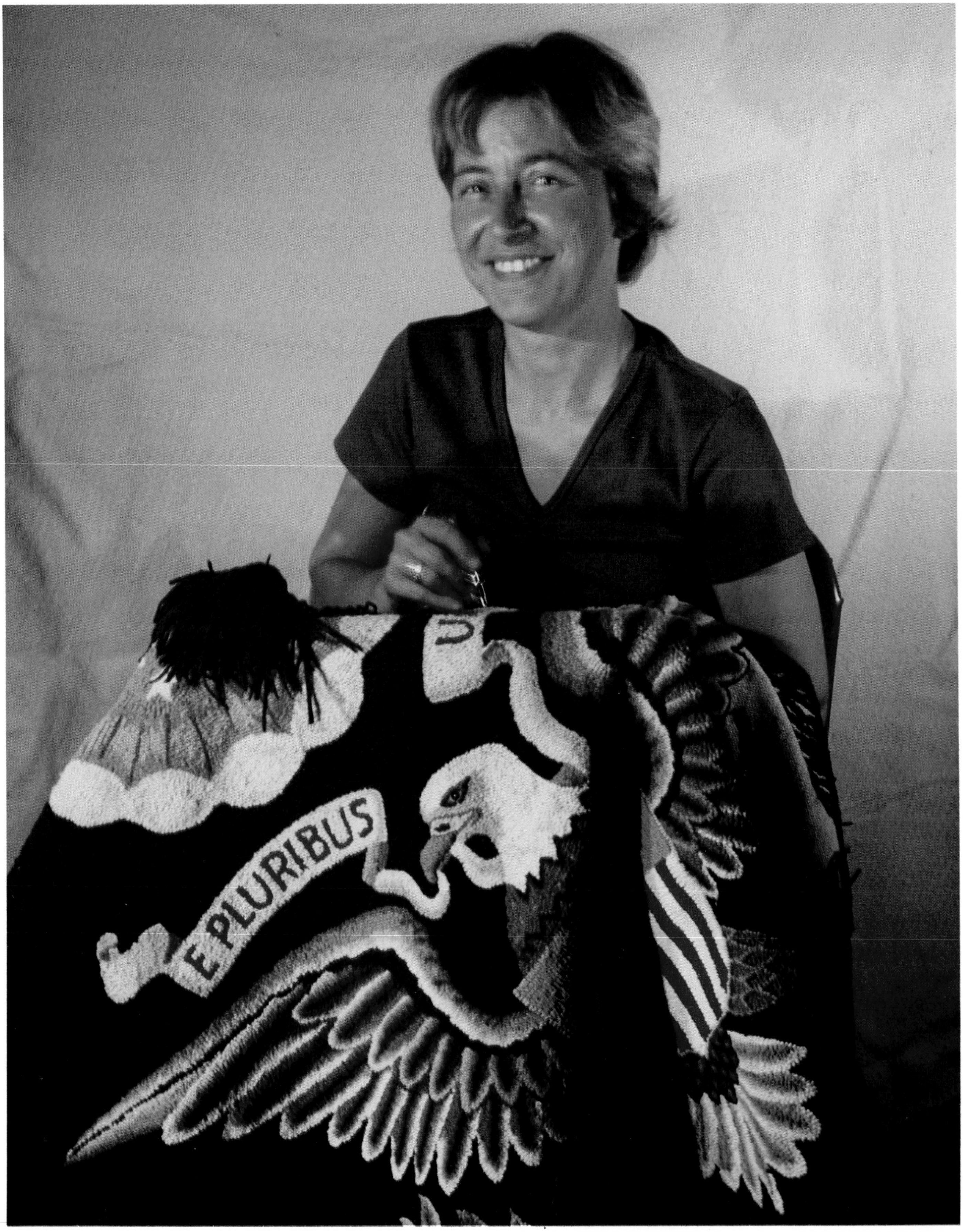

Mary E. Philbrick at work on a 45″ round Presidential seal.
Courtesy of Mary E. Philbrick. Photo by Robert Moshimer

Tiffany's

Marjorie Stafford, display and interior design coordinator for the Boston branch of Tiffany and Company, called me in September, 1991 to discuss using hooked rugs for an in-store presentation. She wished to feature farm house furniture and hooked rugs in conjunction with a sales promotion of fine china. The Tiffany name has always been synonymous with luxury and wealth. Naturally I was quite pleased to offer my assistance.

From my inventory she chose a grouping of antique and semi-antique hooked rugs. The selection included an area-size oval with a floral and scroll design, circa 1880; a Frost pattern of ducks in the marsh, circa 1880; a folk art scene with men and oxen at work, circa 1940; and for table top display, a round Grenfell mat depicting starfish, sea urchins and Northern flowers, circa 1920. Table, chairs and cupboard were on loan courtesy of Wenham Cross Antiques, Newbury Street, Boston.

With an ease known to those of innate talent, Marjorie Stafford coordinated place settings of porcelain, simple furnishings and handmade rugs into room-like vignettes. Tiffany customers were treated not only to the gleam of sterling and the sparkle of exquisite crystal and china but to the charm of country furniture and the lure of hooked rugs.

During the fall of 1991, Tiffany and Company of Copley Place in Boston featured hooked rugs and country furniture for an in-store promotion of fine china. The scroll and floral rug beneath the farm table was hooked from a variety of textiles. Circa 1880. The small hooked rug of ducks is from a Frost pattern, No. 17. Circa 1880. *Courtesy of Tiffany and Company*

Full view of the oval rug displayed by Tiffany and Company. From the early 1900s until his death in 1938, "Hooked Rug Magnate"Ralph W. Burham of Ipswich, Massachusetts poised for many of his advertising photographs on a hooked rug similar to the one pictured. 6′ 3″ x 9′ 3″. Circa 1880.

Amidst the glitter of diamonds and gold, a simple country cupboard holds kitchen ware and pieces of Tiffany porcelain. The folk art hooked rug of farmers and oxen echos the colors of the painted cupboard and the objects placed upon its shelves. *Courtesy of Tiffany and Company*

Full view of the folk art farmer and oxen hooked rug. Note enlarged leaves and bird atop the roof. Made on Prince Edward Island. Circa 1940. 28″ x 40″.

Naomi Stopher appropriately framed her Tiffany peacock with a border of stained glass. 1991. 16″ x 42″. *Photo courtesy of Naomi Stopher*

The Tiffany Studios of New York were resposible for creating exquisite stained windows and lamps during the early 1900s. Nancy Elliott of Georgia recently hooked this landscape fashioned after a Tiffany stained glass window. *Photo courtesy of Nancy Elliott*

7 Hooked Art

Most hooked rugs leave their maker's hands and are placed upon the floor to be seen only by those who travel within the household. It is often an unappreciative audience that views the hand-made carpets, one that takes little interest in the labor of love cushioning their steps. But rugs hooked by the gifted hands of artist Mary Sheppard Burton do not go unnoticed. They earn scores of blue ribbons and merit the attention of museum curators.

Rug hooking was a family tradition. In the 1950's Mary began to enjoy the craft that both her maternal and paternal great-grandmothers had used to warm drafty floors. With strips of wool fabric cut from outgrown children's clothing Mary brought to life the folk art designs she drew, scenes that portray the things in life she held dear. What followed are years of intensive study devoted to all aspects of design and color.

Rug hooking artist Mary Sheppard Burton and friend are pictured with "Kountry Korner Kapers," a room size rug she designed and hooked. *Photo courtesy of Mary Sheppard Burton*

The cumulative results of her efforts distinguish Mary Sheppard Burton as a master rug hooker. Her work is among the permanent collection of the Smithsonian Institution, has been shown by museums such as The Renwick Museum in Washington, D.C., and was recently featured at a gala opening at John Wanamaker's in Philadelphia. Mary has taught rug hooking and lectured throughout the United States, Canada and in Japan. From her Sign o' the Hook Studio in Germantown, Maryland she works on a commission basis, designing a limited number of rug patterns for others to hook. Mary Sheppard Burton has done much to promote rug hooking as an art form. The merit of one's work can often be judged by the company it keeps!

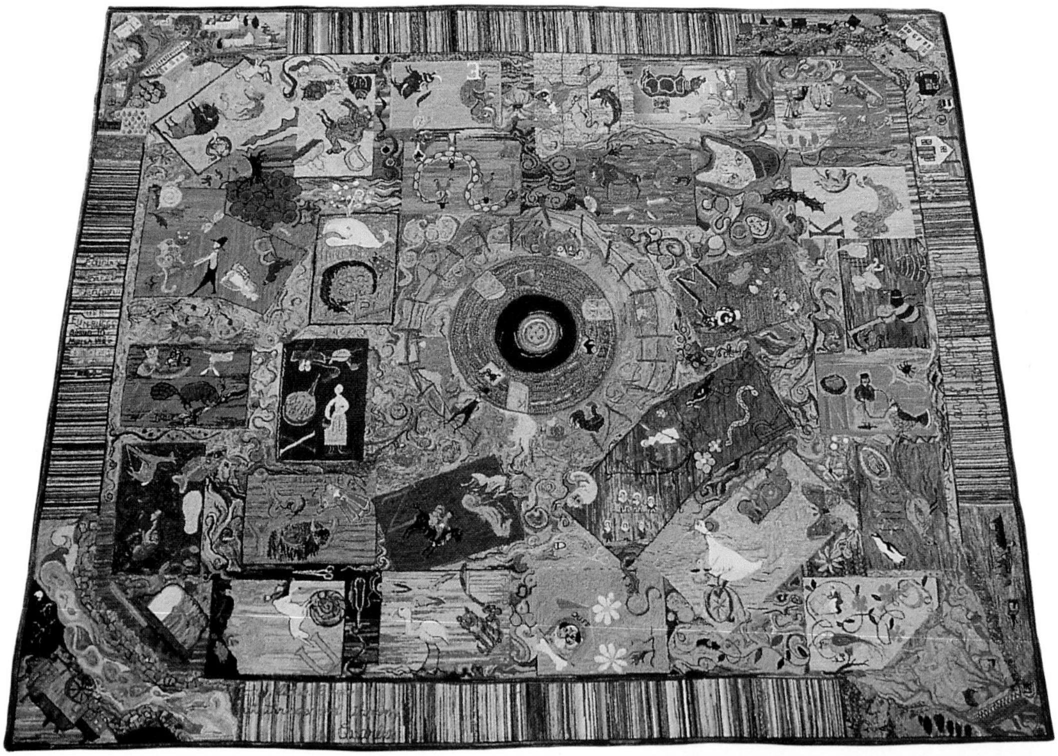

The design for "Kountry Korner Kapers" was adapted from the Shaker children's alphabet used for poetry. One must read the "critters" in proper order to have them rhyme. Each corner of the room size rug is different and depicts life as the Shakers knew it from 1850 to 1870. The pattern also includes personal mementos that Mary holds dear; a gift of a loaf of bread, scissors, hook, a favorite cat, etc. The 9′ 11″ x 11′ 9″ rug hooked of wool fabrics on a linen foundation took two years and eleven months to complete. *Photo courtesy of Mary Sheppard Burton*

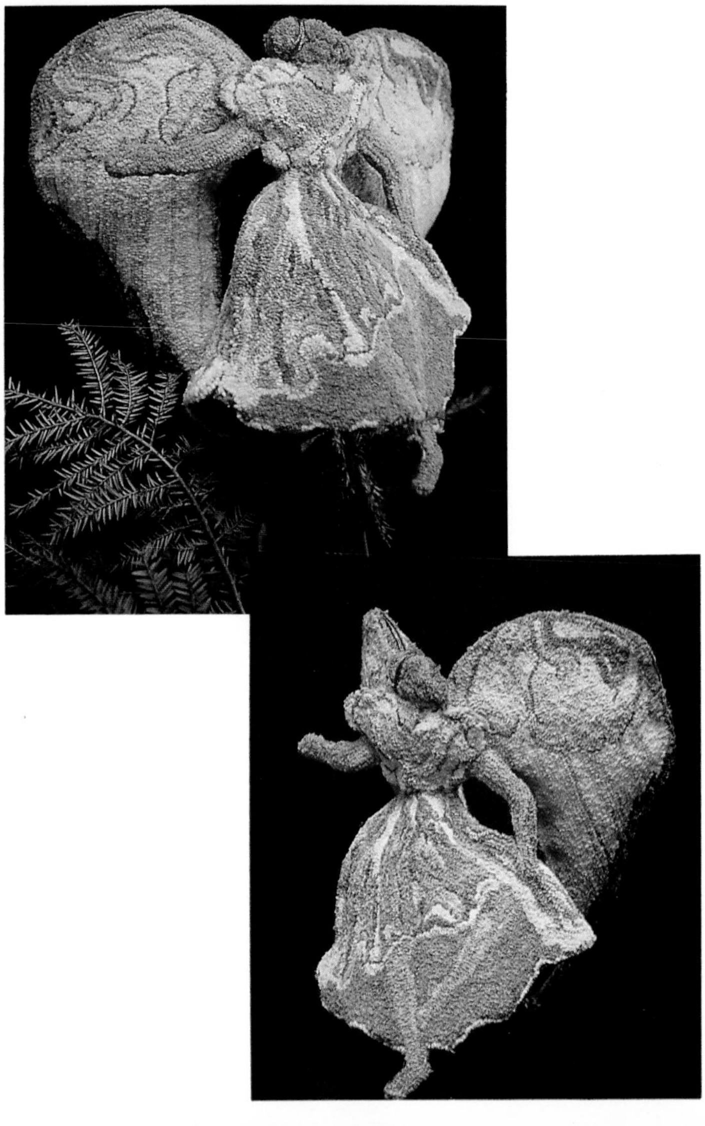

Mary Sheppard Burton's "Tree Top Angel" is among the Christmas Tree Collection at the Smithsonian Institution in Washington, D.C. She designed, dyed the wool fabric, and worked the ornament using a linen foundation and an ultra-fine hook. Approximately 15″ high. *Photo courtesy of Mary Sheppard Burton*

Back view of the "Tree Top Angel" shows the intricate detail of her wings. *Photo courtesy of Mary Sheppard Burton*

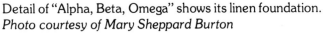

Detail of "Alpha, Beta, Omega" shows its linen foundation. *Photo courtesy of Mary Sheppard Burton*

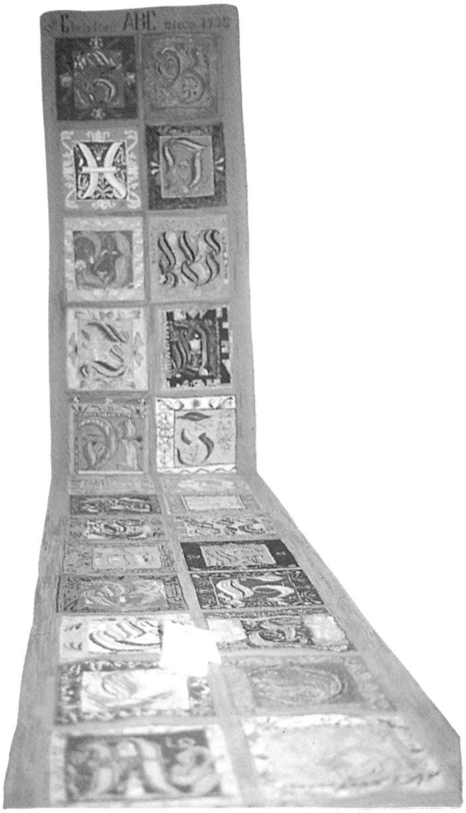

The design for this runner was inspired by one of the most famous books printed in America. The Ephrata Clositer alphabet was printed by the Brothers of Ephrata (Pennsylvania), but drawn by several of the Sisters of the Writing School. Original black on white drawings were done with pen and ink. The "Alpha, Beta, Omega" runner has won many ribbons and claimed several Best of Show awards. 28″ x 13′. *Photo courtesy of Mary Sheppard Burton*

Detail of "Alpha, Beta, Omega." The monks allowed Mary to visit their cloister and study the 18th century alphabet book. Original designs were worked with hairline quill pens. *Photo courtesy of Mary Sheppard Burton*

Detail of "Alpha, Beta, Omega"; the letter "F." *Photo courtesy of Mary Sheppard Burton*

Detail of a portion of the "Hands Across the Border" stair risers. *Photo courtesy of Mary Sheppard Burton*

"Hands Across the Border" is a set of thirty-six individual stair risers. Mary Sheppard Burton's design illustrates Maryland history; events relating to colonial times through 1920. Special attention was given to the social documentation of habits, costumes and transportation throughout the periods. Each riser is 4″ x 28″. *Photo courtesy of Mary Sheppard Burton*

Detail of an individual riser. 4″ x 28″. *Photo courtesy of Mary Sheppard Burton*

Detail of an individual riser that documents American costumes over a two hundred year period. *Photo courtesy of Mary Sheppard Burton*

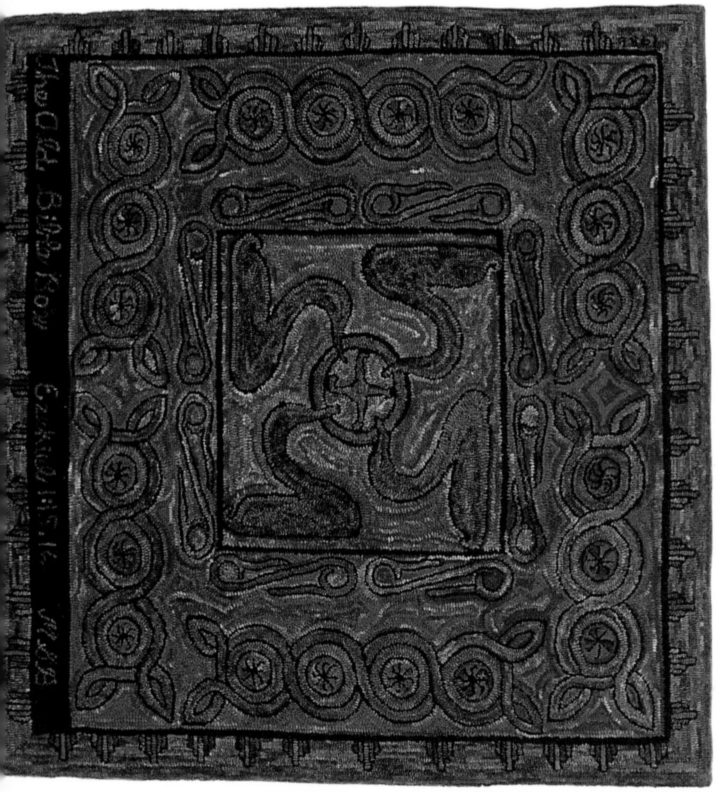

The design for this commissioned piece was taken from a hand-carved Bible box dating back to the time of the Pilgrims. This wall hanging designed and hooked by Mary Sheppard Burton is on diplay in the lobby of the World Baptist Alliance Headquarters in McLean, Virginia. A special ceremony was held to commemorate the artist's work. 40″ x 40″. *Photo courtesy of Mary Sheppard Burton*

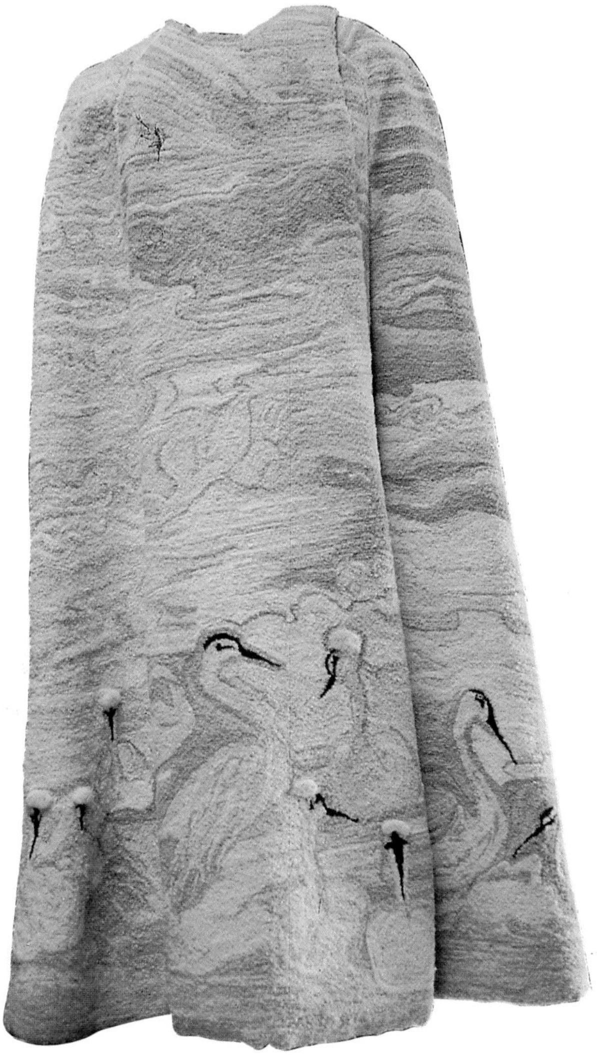

"A Mantle To Remember" is a cape designed and hooked by Mary Sheppard Burton. The work was inspired by Sadako, a Japanese child who died from leukemia as a result of an atomic blast. Japanese legend states that if you fold a thousand paper cranes your soul will survive forever. At Sadako's death, she was buried with the 634 paper cranes she had folded plus the nearly 400 which her loving classmates folded. A monument to her memory stands in Hiroshima Peace Park. Every year on August 6th many thousand paper cranes are folded and placed around the monument in memory of a child's courage and love. *Photo courtesy of Mary Sheppard Burton*

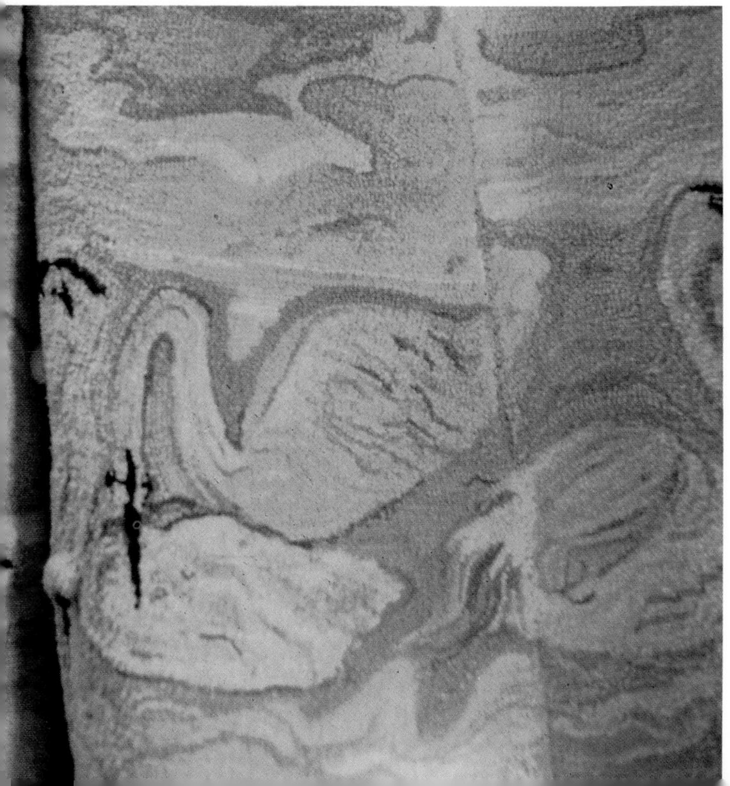

Detail of "A Mantle to Remember." Tapestry hooked on 22 thread count linen. *Photo courtesy of Mary Sheppard Burton*

"In the Garden" designed and hooked by Mary Sheppard Burton is a choice minature. Hooked on 22 thread count linen using an ultra-fine hook, there are approximately 360 loops per square inch. 9" x 12". *Photo courtesy of Mary Sheppard Burton*

In April of 1993, the John Wanamaker department store in Philadelphia, Pennsylvania, presented an exhibit of the works of Mary Sheppard Burton. Hooked rug authorities Joan and Robert Moshimer of Kennebunkport, Maine were on hand for the opening clelbration. *Photo by Susan L. Smidt*

Displayed with the tools of her trade are Mary Sheppard Burton's hooked "Chapeau" and "Spats." *Photo by Susan L. Smidt*

The artist hooked a rose for the cover of this hat box. Beside it rests a hat decorated with a hooked leaf. *Photo by Susan L. Smidt*

Hooked Art

The technique of hooking is an easily mastered skill. A series of loops are formed by pulling thin strips of fabric through a loosely woven foundation. All hooked rugs, antique or newly made, of simple design or elaborate, share this essential process, though the particulars may vary. Early rug makers of the 1860's hooked strips of rag into a burlap sack base. Modern rug hookers work upon specially woven foundations of jute, linen or cotton fashioning loops from top quality wool fabric. Commercial dyes now enable ruggers to tint fabrics a full spectrum of rainbow colors that their forerunners could only dream of using. Modern improvements in frame designs help to simplify the mechanics of the hooking process.

Though the hooking tool and method of hooking has not changed essentially in over 100 years, the reasons for continuing the art have altered drastically. Today's efficient heating systems and machine made carpeting eliminate the need of crafting rugs to insulate cold floors. Today's men and women hook for pleasure.

Rug hooking can be an avenue for artistic expression. Hooking artists challenge their abilities and attempt to create different effects in their work through the use of color and/or texture. The objective is to hook unique works of art, compositions for the mind to contemplate and the eye to enjoy.

Other hookers relish the challenge of trying to reproduce beloved masterpieces. With a palette of subtly shaded wools, hooking Rembrandts mimic the qualities of oil paintings, water colors, etchings, illustrations, sculptures; all inspire the hooking artist.

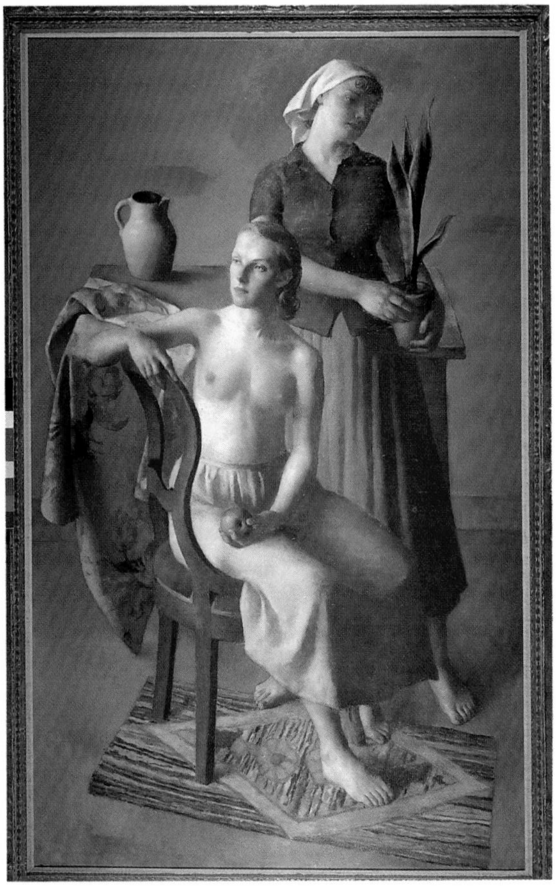

"Morning Light" by Robert Brackman is a figure study of two females, his wife and a model who appears in several other of his works. The undated oil was painted in Connecticut between 1938 and 1942. Brackman was born in Odessa, Russia, in 1898. He died a citizen of the United States in 1979. The artist chose to place a hooked rug at the feet of the seated figure. 50" x 80". *Photo courtesy of John Pence Gallery*

Today's hooking artists have access to a variety of top quality materials and tools.

"Mrs. Williams" by John Hoppner (1758-1810) hangs in the Tate Gallery in London. Artist Elsie Myserian fashioned her hooked portrait after the Hoppner painting. 13″ x 19″.

Detail reveals the delicate shading of the hooked portrait.

"Lou Ann" hooked by Lou Carson is an adaptation of a Goetze portrait. 22″ x 27″. *Photo courtesy of Jeanne Edwards*

An illustration from the children's book *The Rhyming Rainbow* by Cicely Mary Barker. Hooked by Elsie Myserian in the 1980s. 13″ x 20″.

"Geranium Fairy" from *Fairies of the Garden* by Cicely Mary Barker. Hooked by Elsie Myserian in the 1980s. 20″ x 24″.

"Lavender Fairy" from *Flower Fairies of the Garden* by Cicely Mary Barker. Hooked by Elsie Myserian in the 1980s. 20″ x 24″.

Hooked reproduction of a portrait of George Washington. 20" x 24". *Courtesy of Joan Moshimer. Photo by Robert Moshimer*

"Stop at the Inn" was hooked by Mary E. Hargrove in 1991. Pearl K. McGown pattern. 25" x 40". *Photo courtesy of Mary E. Hargrove*

Adapted from a Currier and Ives print. Hooked by Ethel Bruce.

Artist Janet West announces in bold letters the presence of her hooked piece. 1991. 30″ x 31″. *Photo by John West*

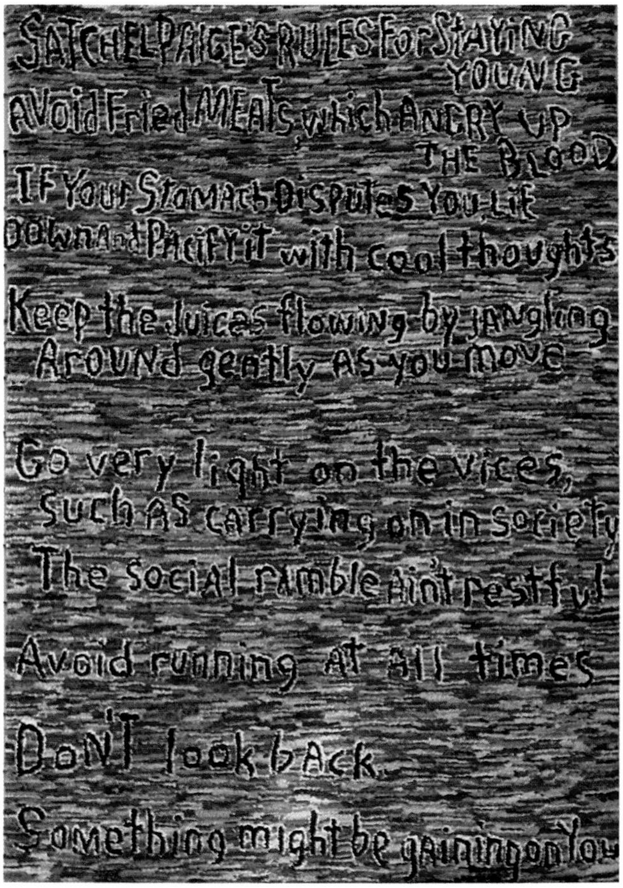

A visit to the Baseball Hall of Fame in Cooperstown, New York, inspired Janet West to hook "Satchel Paige's Rules for Staying Young." Paige (1906?-1982), an Afro-American baseball pitcher, was allowed to enter the major leagues in 1948 despite prejudice against black players. He was elected to the Baseball Hall of Fame in 1971. 62″ x 88″. *Photo by John West*

Wool reproduction of "The Cat." The original painting (circa 1840) is in the collection of the National Gallery of Art, Washington, D.C. Hooked by Janet West. 1990. 27″ x 41″. *Photo by John West*

A bright-eyed and ruby-lipped female holds the flowers of spring. Hooked by Janet West. 1990. 13" x 46". *Photo courtesy of John West*

While an inmate at the Bedford Hills Correctional Facility in New York, Inez Nathaniel Walker began to draw small and simple compositions. With time, the drawings became larger and more elaborate. Her work has been displayed in galleries throughout the United States and has earned her recognition as an American black folk artist. This image was hooked by Janet West. 1992. 29" x 42". *Photo by John West*

A collection of Janet West's hooked art waits to be unrolled. *Photo by John West*

Mary MacLaren Thomson designed and hooked this fireboard of tulips and daffodils. 1991-1992. 30" x 40".

Detail of Mary MacLaren Thomson's work shows the subtle changes of color used in shading her composition.

"Irises" designed and hooked by Connie Fletcher. 26" x 34".
Photo courtesy of Connie Fletcher

Fumiyo Hachisuka accompanied her husband on his eight year work assignment in Canada. One day, feeling rather homesick for her home in Japan, Fumiyo visited a Canadian public library. There she became interested in a hooked rug display presented by hooking teacher Fannie Sinclair. Under the guidance of the Canadian instructor, the hooking talents of the young Japanese woman flourished. Fumiyo returned to Tokyo in 1985. She exhibits her work, teaches the craft and continues to spread the joy of rug hooking in a land where very little was known about the North American art. Fumiyo's "Lady Liberty" was among other hooked pieces exhibited at the American Fair in a Tokyo department store. *Photo courtesy of Mary Sheppard Burton*

Japanese rug hooking artist Fumiyo Hachisuka has given great depth to an American treasure, the Statue of Liberty. *Photo courtesy of Fumiyo Hachisuka*

"Fireworks" by Fumiyo Hachisuka was hooked with the silk material of her grandmother's kimono. *Photo courtesy of Fumiyo Hachisuka*

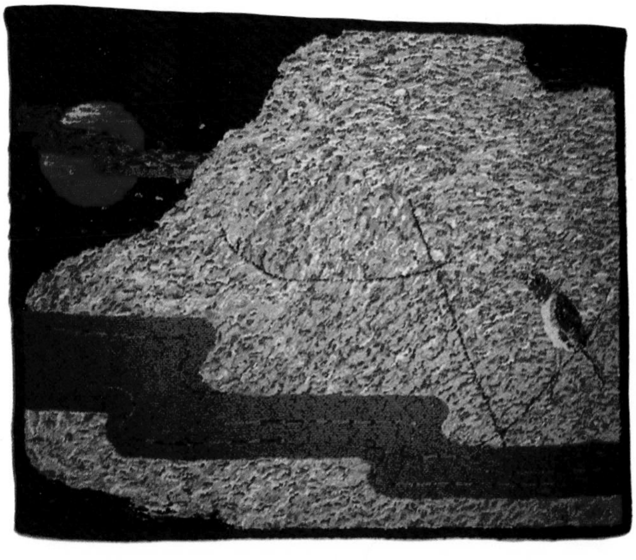

"Spring" an original work by Fumiyo Hachisuka was hooked with strips of silk cut from an old kimono. *Photo courtesy of Fumiyo Hachisuka*

"Bamboo" by Fumiyo Hachisuka. The original design was hooked with silk and eight value swatches of wool fabric hand dyed by the artist. Completed 1991. 54″ x 78″. *Photo courtesy of Fumiyo Hachisuka*

"Butterflies" by Fumiyo Hachisuka. *Photo courtesy of Fumiyo Hachisuka*

An aquatint by Cornelius B. Hulsart which was engraved, printed and colored by J. Hill and published by Hulsart in 1835 "...for sale at the Office of the Seamen's Friend Society, 82 Nassau St, New York." The print is dedicated: "To Messrs. N. & W. W. Billings Merchants of New London, this Print is respectfully inscribed by Cornelius B. Hulsart who lost an arm on board their Ship Superior while engaged in Whale Fishery in the Pacific Ocean." The print is in the collection of the Kendall Whaling Museum, Sharon, Massachusetts

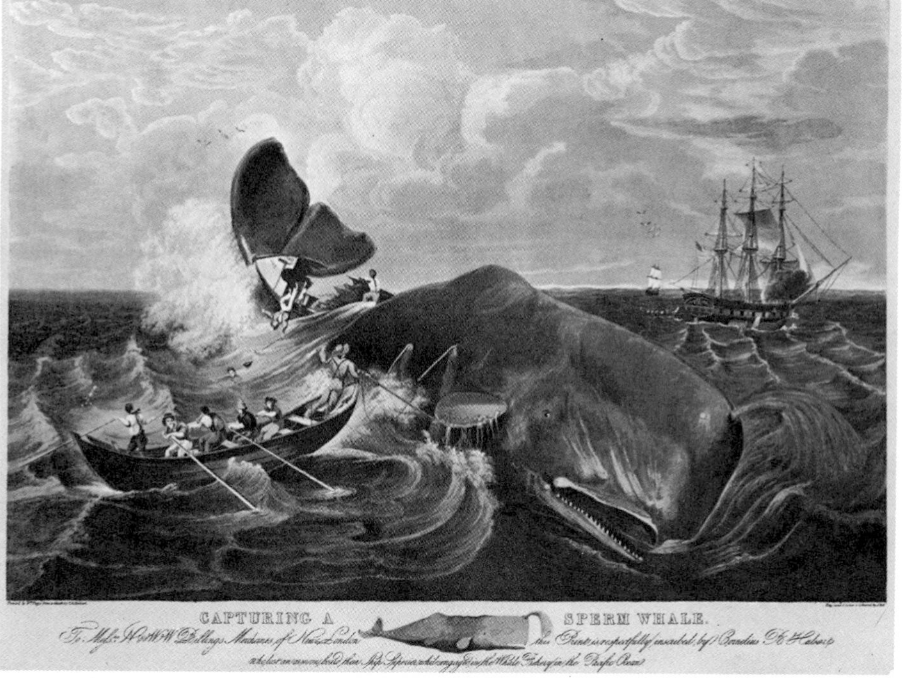

The acquatint "Capturing A Sperm Whale" served as inspiration for Virginia G. Sheldon's hooked tapestry. 1981. 35" x 52". The artist's work was exhibited at the Kendall Whaling Museum in Sharon, Massachusetts.

"Old Salts and the Cat." Hooked in Nova Scotia. Circa 1900. 39" x 49". *Courtesy of the Kent Collection*

In addition to offering a large inventory of hooked rugs, antique dealer Ralph W. Burnham printed and sold hooked rug patterns and supplies at his Ipswich, Massachusetts, Trading Post. His wife Nellie continued the pattern business after his death, until 1957. Eventually, the rights to the designs were sold. "A vew of Newburyport, Massachusetts, 1847, from Salisbury" was among the Burnham collection of hooked rug patterns. It is a copy of an old print from the now defunct Marine Museum in Boston, Massachusetts. *Courtesy of Annie A. Spring*

Theresa Wells recently hooked the old Burnham pattern of "Newburyport, Massachusetts from Salisbury." The scene portrays the Atlantic coastline town during 1847, when the harbor was a bustling center for seafaring activity. 29" x 60". *Photo courtesy of Theresa Wells*

"Portland Light" in Maine was hooked by Wilma K. Perrin in 1954. From a pattern. 30" x 40". *Courtesy of Beverly J. Darling*

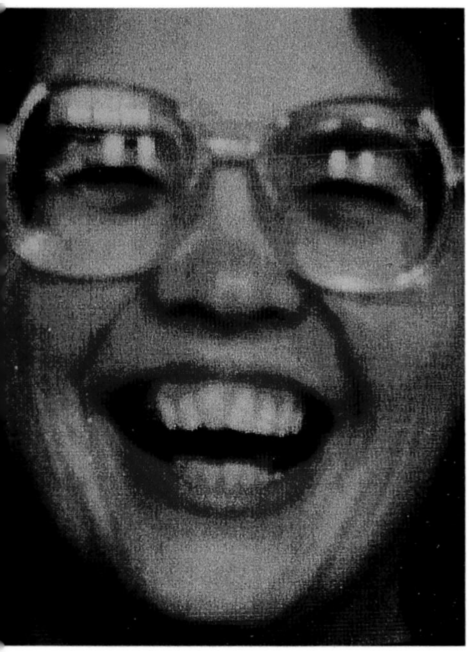

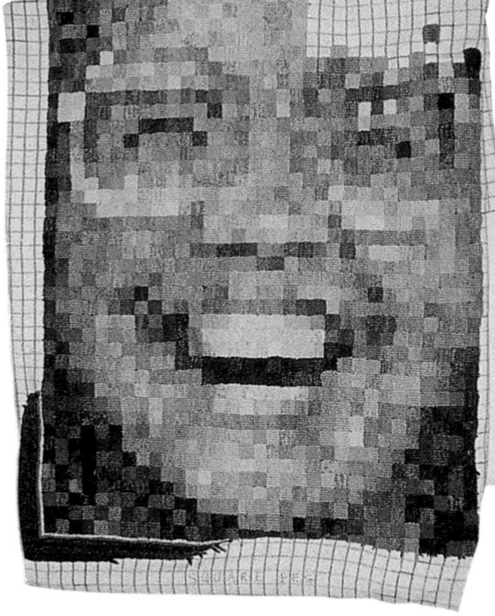

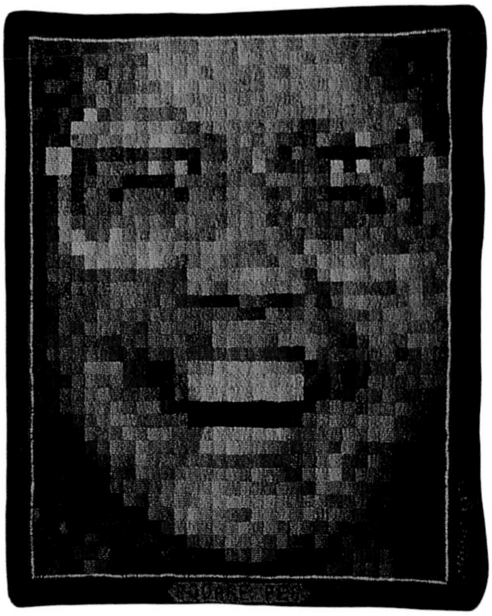

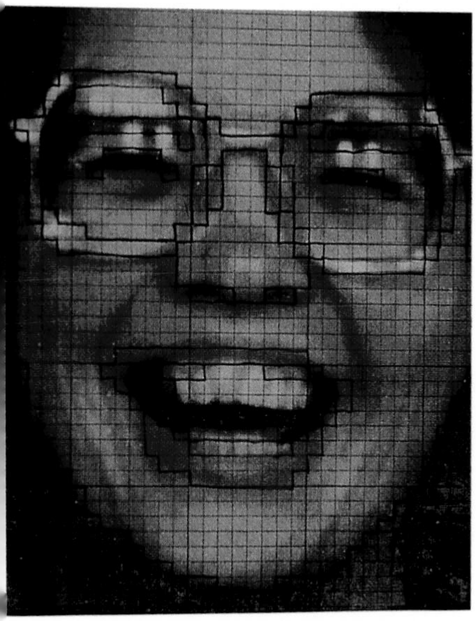

"Square Peg," a self-portrait by Massachusetts rug hooking artist and teacher Peg Irish. The composition was worked in ½" squares of color, inspired by the quilts of Marcia Ente. It is 32 squares wide by 40 squares long (1280 squares total). Each square contains thirty-six hooked loops. *Photo courtesy of Peg Irish*

"Elm Glen Farm," by New Hampshire rug hooking artist Ann Winterling. The landscape depicts the home of Ann's beloved Aunt Helen. As a young child during the early 1930s, Ann was a regular visitor at the farm. Aunt Helen spun wool from her sheep into knitting yarn, but what impressed young Ann most was her aunt's skill at rug hooking. *Photo by Garth Winterling*

"Raspberry Festival," hooked by Ann Winterling from a pattern designed by her daughter Heather Erskine. The composition was inspired by a family pet, Fierce Bad Rabbit, who always managed to escape from his cage and go bounding away towards the raspberry bushes. 30" x 36". *Photo by Garth Winterling*

Detail of "Elm Glen Farm." *Photo courtesy of Garth Winterling*

"Sweet William," designed by Heather Erskine and hooked by Ann Winterling. Both Ann and her daughter loved to draw and paint scenes of their family farm in New Hampshire. Sweet William was a favorite young steer who often posed as a model for the rural artists. 27" x 44". *Photo by Garth Winterling*

O BLESSED BEAUTIFUL LAND

"Canterbury Shaker Village,"designed and hooked by Ann Winterling. As a volunteer at the Canterbury Shaker Village in New Hampshire, Ann came to know and love the last two Eldresses; Bertha Lindsay, Lead Minister in the Shaker world and Eldress Gertrude. The simplicity of the piece reflects the plain and simple life led by the Shakers. Pictured are three of the many buildings that remain in the village today; the meeting house, the dwelling house and school. *O Blessed Beautiful Land* is the title of a hymn sung by the school children. Bertha and Gertrude are pictured wearing their favorite clothes. They stand on Meeting House Lane, which is lined with maple trees. The Shakers took in orphans, children who had been abused, or any person needing help. When Bertha came to Canterbury Village, a maple sapling was given to each orphan brought into the community. The tree was named for the child it was given to. The young maple's care became the responsibility of that child. A small raised herb garden is included in the scene to commemorate the Shakers work with seeds and herbs. The Shakers had the first mail order seed business in the country. Trees to the left represent their aboretum, the first in the country, begun by Elder Henry Blinn in the 1800s. The circular garden is one that had fallen into neglect. Presently there is an effort underway to restore the circular garden once worked by Eldress Bertha. A larger and more detailed version of this rug was presented to Bertha. Although blind, she loved the hooked rug and enjoyed telling its story to visitors. 21" x 24". *Photo by Garth Winterling*

Hooking artist and teacher Betty McClentic works on a rug she designed. The pattern was inspired by the Arts and Crafts Movement (1897-1914), which Betty has thoroughly researched. A Frost pattern hooked rug (circa 1880) is displayed behind the artist.

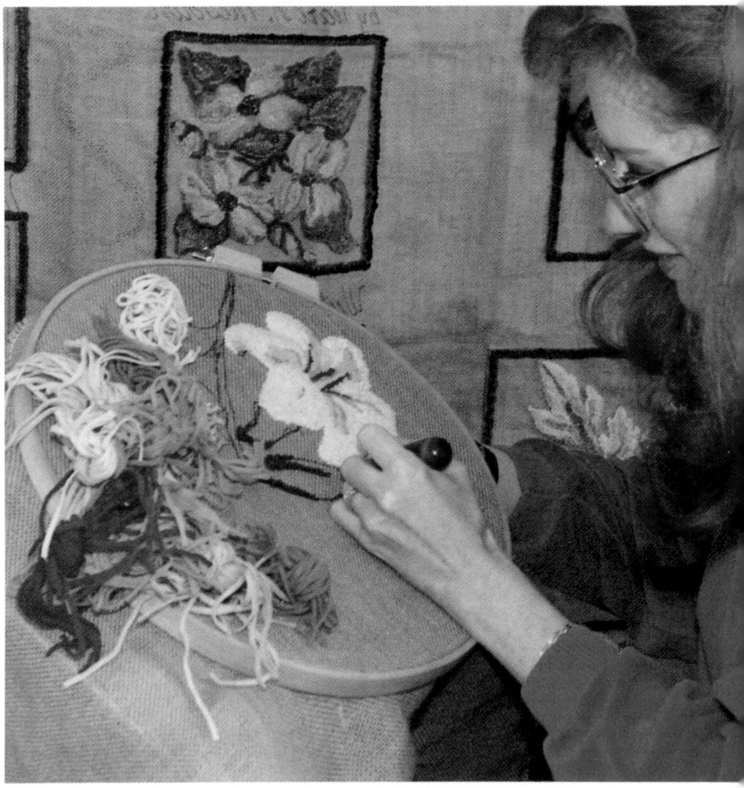

Interior decorator and consultant Susan E. Schaefer works on an original floral design hooked rug. Her backdrop is a 1940s Pearl K. McGown teacher's sampler.

"Panama Primitive," designed and hooked by Barbara Ham Bancroft. 29" x 39". *Photo courtesy of Marion N. Ham*

Art teacher Janine Denizard Saint-Louis enjoys hooking an Oriental design .

Roslyn Logsdon

The physical vantage point from which hooked rugs are viewed has also greatly changed. Many that sat on the floor for years have been swept clean and hung upon walls. This newfound appreciation is due to the growing popularity of hooked rugs, a long overdue respect for the craft, scarcity of antique hooked rugs and an unwillingness among modern hookers to part with their labors of love. The combination of these factors has caused the monetary value of hooked rugs to rise.

The public is beginning to perceive hooking as a true art form and not just a craft enjoyed by those of modest means. Roslyn Logsdon is among the artists responsible for this change in attitude. As a painter, Roslyn turned to rug hooking as "a temporary escape" from her hectic schedule. She enjoyed the feel of the fibers and look of the hooked surface. Years of experimenting with the medium has enabled her to achieve with wool material the images that she wants to paint. Tweed, plaid, heather, solid and hand dyed fabrics bring additional texture to her work. Use of color is controlled. The studies hooked by Roslyn express relationships between people, people and architectural elements, and architectural elements by themselves.

Her work has been shown at galleries and museums across the United States. She maintains a studio at the Montpelier Cultural Arts Center in Laurel, Maryland. Roslyn Logsdon portrays scenes that provoke thought and jar memories. The captured moments that this artist so proficiently hooks were never meant to cushion the underside of a shoe.

"Backyard Conversation" by Roslyn Logsdon. 1990. 21" x 28". *Photo courtesy of Roslyn Logsdon*

"Outdoor Cafe: Two People with Book" by Roslyn Logsdon. 1992. 21" x 24". *Photo courtesy of Roslyn*

"Outdoor Cafe: Conversation With Dog" by Roslyn Logsdon. 1992. 24" x 35". *Photo courtesy of Roslyn Logsdon*

"Outdoor Cafe: Man with Teapot" by Roslyn Logsdon. 1992. 17" x 24". *Photo courtsey of Roslyn Logsdon*

"Baseball Joe" by Roslyn Logsdon. 1990. 7" x 13". *Photo courtesy of Roslyn Logsdon*

"Sliding Home" by Roslyn Logsdon. 1991. 27" x 35". *Photo courtesy of Roslyn Logsdon*

"Italian Conversation" by Roslyn Logsdon. 1989. 30″ x 39″. *Photo courtesy of Roslyn Logsdon*

"Woman with Book" by Roslyn Logsdon. 1990. 15″ x 21″. *Photo courtesy of Roslyn Logsdon*

"Laurel Porch" by Roslyn Logsdon. 1990. 14″ x 18″. *Photo courtesy of Roslyn Logsdon*

"Christ Church College, Oxford" by Roslyn Logsdon. 1988. 20" x 34". *Photo courtesy of Roslyn Logsdon*

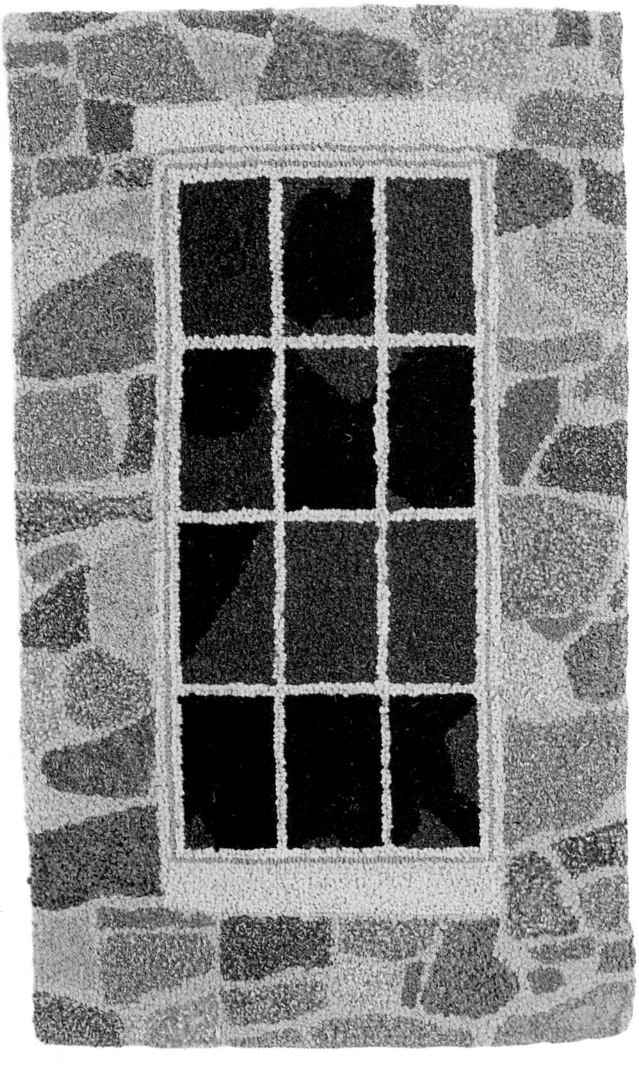

"Window: Avondale Mill" by Roslyn Logsdon. 1990. 14" x 22". *Photo courtesy of Roslyn Logsdon*

"Windows: Montpelier" by Roslyn Logsdon. 1990. 14" x 18". *Photo courtesy of Roslyn Logsdon*

Susan L. Smidt

Among those rug hooking artists not afraid of marching to a different drummer is Susan Smidt [formerly Goldberg]. Known in the rug hooking world for her unique abstracts, Susan continues to hook in the same manner as those who crafted rugs in the late 1800's. New and different is the medium she hooks with. In conjunction with the John Smidt Company of Peabody, Massachusetts, Susan has perfected the process of bonding metallic fibers to wool material. When thinly cut and hooked, the marriage of a traditional fabric with shimmering laminate produces a pleasing iridescent effect. *Illusion* metallic wool is available to the public upon request. One begins to wonder what Susan Smidt will think of next.

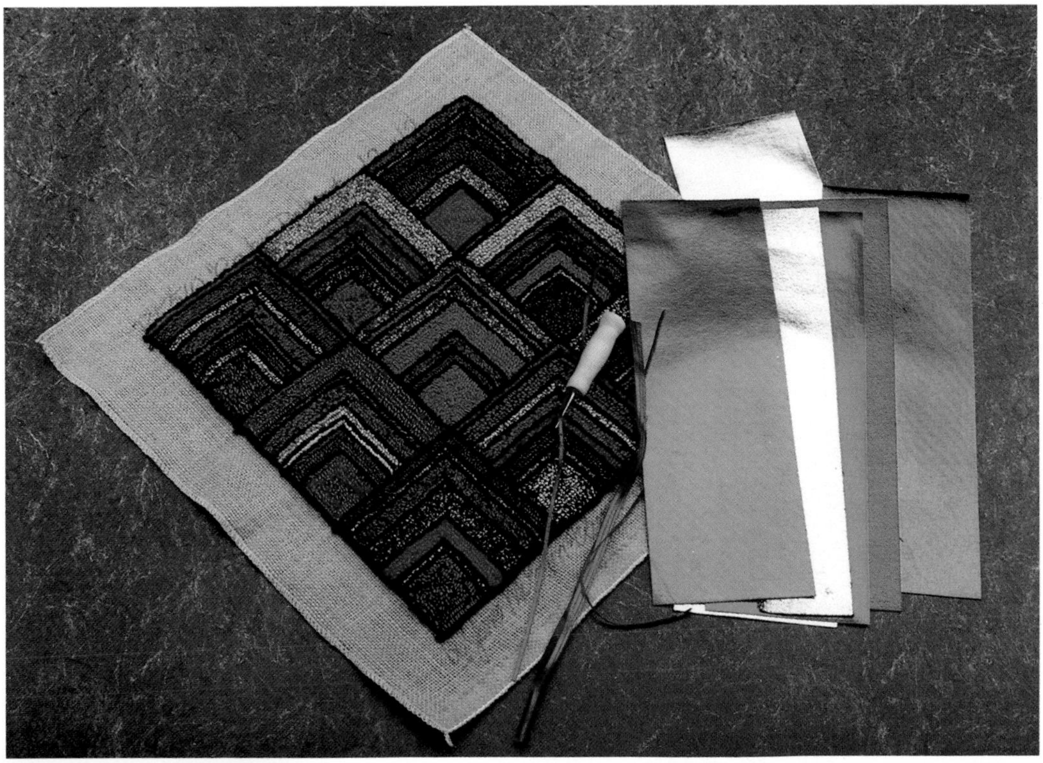

Susan L. Smidt hooks with *Illusion* metallic wool. The shimmering laminate is fused to wool fabric. Jane McGown Flynn pattern. 1993. 12" x 12".

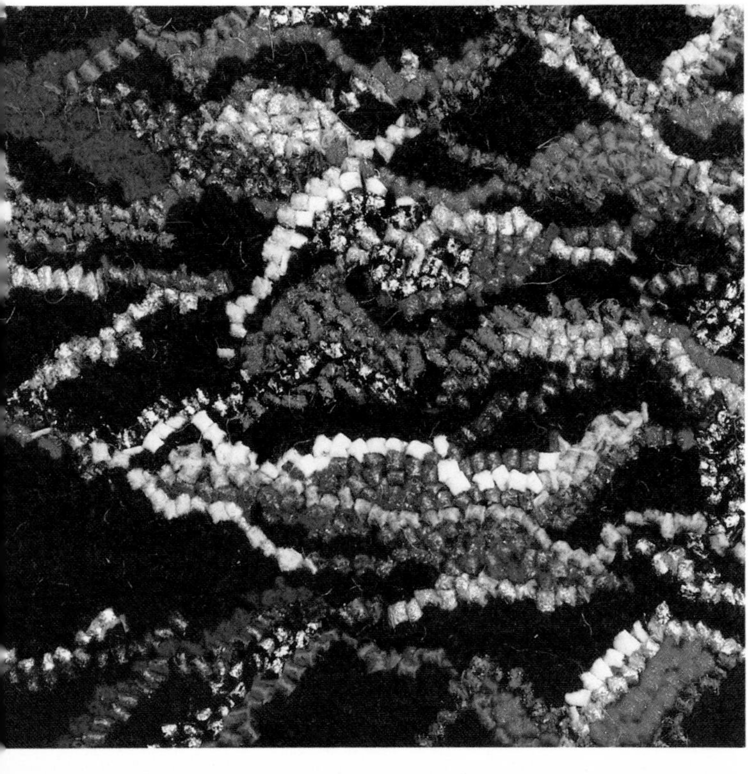

"Abstract Seaweed Miniature,"an original design hooked by Susan L. Smidt using *Illusion* wool. 1993. 6" x 8".

The iridescence of metallic wool brings a mystical quality to this Arabian scene. Hooked by Susan L. Smidt. Jane McGown Flynn pattern. 1992. 8" x 36".

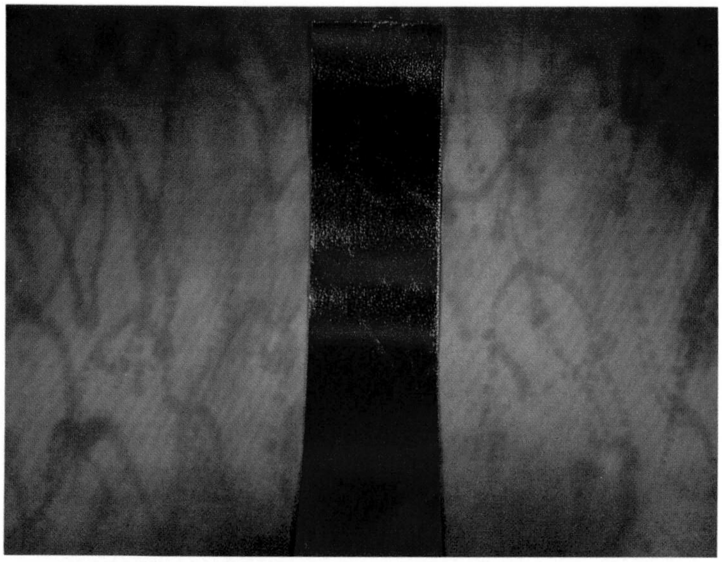

Hand dyed wool fabric and companion *Illusion. Photo courtesy of Peg Irish*

"Sunflower," a pattern by Joan Moshimer was hooked by Susan L. Smidt with *Illusion*. 1992. Diameter 15".

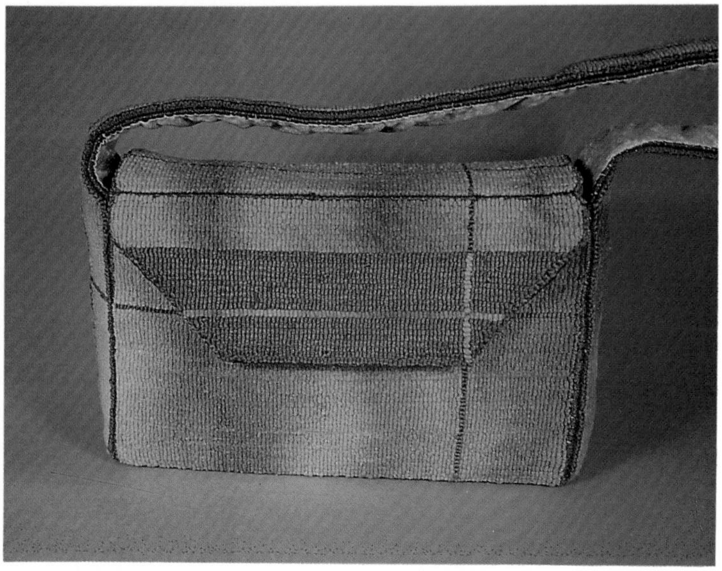

"Sunset Handbag" by Peg Irish. Hooking artist and teacher Peg Irish creates with iridescent blue *Illusion* and wool fabric she hand dyes. *Photo courtesy of Peg Irish*

"Currents Handbag" by Peg Irish. Gold metallic *Illusion* and hand dyed wool are hooked to mimic the movement of water. *Photo courtesy of Peg Irish*

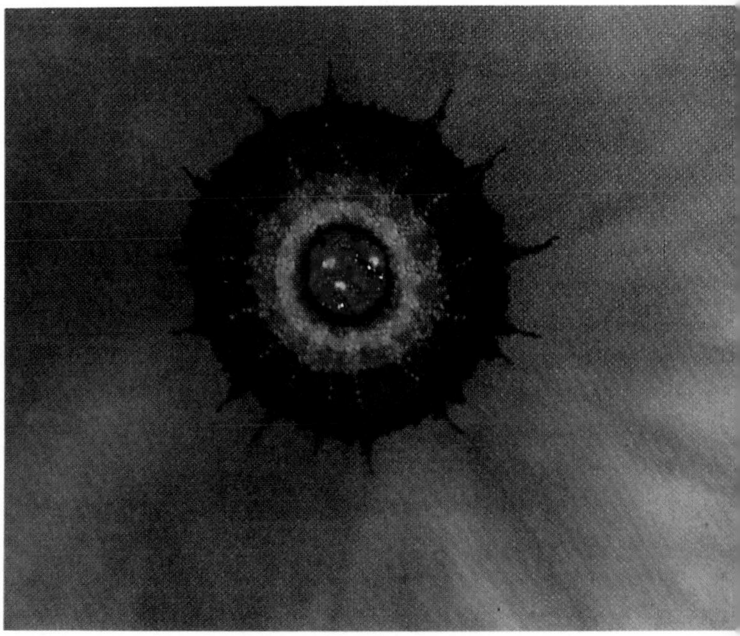

"Landform" by Peg Irish. Red *Illusion* metallic wool was used to fashion the "magma" in the center of the volcano-like compostion. *Photo courtesy of Peg Irish*

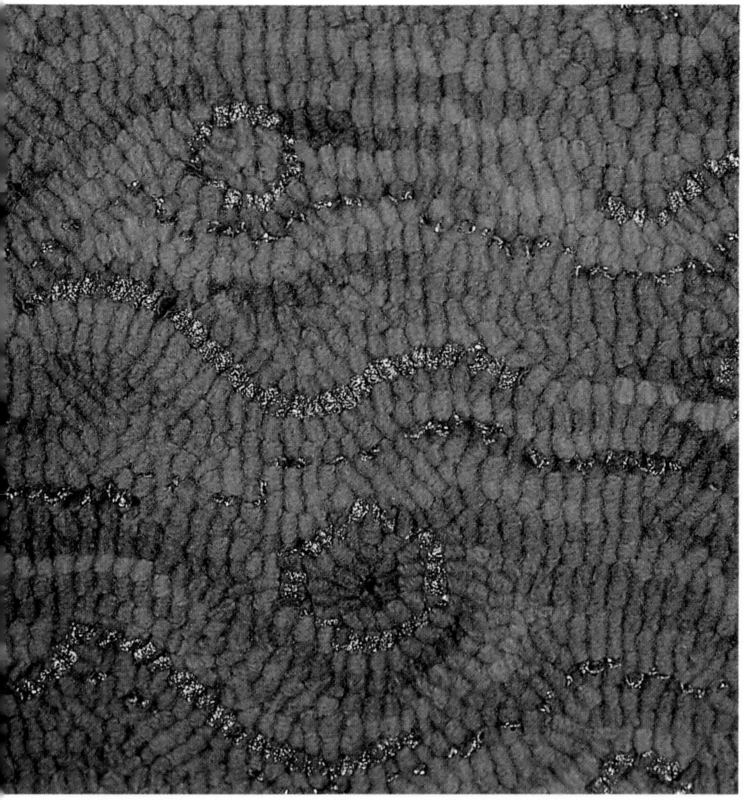

Detail of Peg Irish's "Currents Handbag." *Photo courtesy of Peg Irish*

Mary Paul Wright

Mary Paul Wright had saved a 1950s *Woman's Day* article on rug hooking, and 23 years later (in 1973) took a series of eight lessons from a local teacher. But fancy scrolls and floral designs were not what the gentle lady from Atlanta wanted to hook. Being an artist, Mary Paul Wright was opposed to using the popular printed patterns that the teacher offered; she wanted to design her own rugs. At a time when it was in vogue to hook with the thinnest strips of wool possible, Mary Paul preferred to cut her material just a bit wider.

Feeling that she was somehow different from the other rug makers in the area, Mary Paul chose to create primitive-style hooked rugs without the guidance of a teacher. When shown during the late 1970's at the Atlanta Hookrafters Guild meeting, her original hooked scenes of houses, people and landscapes attracted and intrigued other rug makers. Upon the persistent urging of those who had fashioned the skillfully shaded flowers and elaborate scrolls, Mary Paul Wright began her career as a rug hooking teacher.

Today, from her Atlanta studio, Mary Paul offers three classes per week and is responsible for several successful hooked rug exhibits held at McElreath Hall in Atlanta. Her students demonstrate their craft on a regular basis at the Tullie Smith House maintained by the Atlanta Historical Society. A waiting list of pupils eager to experience the joys of rug hooking attest to Mary Paul's popularity and skill as a teacher. While ensuring that all are thoroughly schooled in the proper techniques of the craft, Mary Paul Wright encourages others to be original, to express their individual tastes and talents.

Rug hooking artist and teacher Mary Paul Wright and fellow hooker Mary Floyd demonstrate their craft at the 1990 Sandy Springs Historical Festival at the Williams-Payne House in Atlanta, Georgia. *Photo courtesy of Mary Paul Wright*

"The Red House" designed and hooked by Mary Paul Wright. The flag is pictured at half-mast; the *Challenger* astronauts were killed the day Mary Paul put the design on the burlap foundation. 1986. 36" x 48". *Photo courtesy of Mary Paul Wright.*

Students of Mary Paul Wright demonstrate rug hooking at the Tullie Smith House in Atlanta, Georgia.

"Hegira" (an Arabic term for "the journey") was designed and hooked by Mary Paul Wright for her sister-in-law Nadene Lord. The rug illustrates landmarks of importance to the family. Spires in the upper left corner represent Kenyon College in Gambier, Ohio. Upper right corner is the Lord home in Gambier and the tower has the call letters of the radio station where in years past Nadene hosted a talk show. The Pinehurst Country Club in Pinehurst, North Carolina is pictured at lower left; site where many happy hours were spent playing tennis and golf. And in the lower left corner, the Lord's retirement home. 1992 . 32″ x 43″. *Photo courtesy of Mary Paul Wright*

"Tennssee Contentment," hooked by Mary Paul Wright was inspired by a magazine photograph. The Smoky Mountains are pictured in the background. 31" x 51". *Photo courtesy of Mary Paul Wright*

"The Peay House," designed and hooked by Mary Paul Wright. 1987. 36" x 48". *Photo courtesy of Mary Paul Wright*

Mary Paul Wright's first attempt at primitive hooking marks the celebration of her daughter's wedding. 24" x 36". *Photo courtesy of Mary Paul Wright*

"Homestead," designed and hooked by Mary Paul Wright. 32" x 49". *Photo courtesy of Mary Paul Wright*

"The Crim House," a commissioned work designed and hooked by Mary Paul Wright. 1989. 36" x 48". *Photo courtesy of Mary Paul Wright*

Fashioned after a photograph in *Antiques Magazine*, "Antique Flower Basket" was hooked by Mary Paul Wright. 1990. 28" x 41". *Photo courtesy of Mary Paul Wright*

"Cedar Hill Farm" was hooked by Dede Bowles, student of Mary Paul Wright. The rug commemorates Dede's circa 1840 home in Barnesville, Georgia. Potato Creek runs in back of the property. To the left of the small barn is a large rock where the lady and original owner of the house taught Bible stories to the children of the slaves that worked on the farm. 1988. *Photo courtesy of Dede Bowles*

Under the guidance of Mary Paul Wright, Elizabeth Rowe designed, cut by hand the strips of wool and hooked "Almost Sunday." 1985. 23" x 27". *Photo courtesy of Elizabeth Rowe*

Her grandson Jeff's kindergarten drawing was copied and hooked by Mary Paul Wright. *Photo courtesy of Mary Paul Wright*

Designed by Mary Paul Wright and hooked by Celia Lockerman. Chances on the hooked rug portraying the Tullie Smith House were sold by the Atlanta Historical Society. Interest in the handiwork generated $600.00 for the foundation. *Photo courtesy of Mary Paul Wright*

"Angela Wescott's House" designed by Lita McCormick and hooked by Angela Wescott. Both are students of Mary Paul Wright. 1991. *Photo courtesy of Mary Paul Wright*

Pat Tritt, under the guidance of Mary Paul Wright, designed and hooked "Shoes" for her granddaughter who loves interesting footwear. 1992. *Photo courtesy of Mary Paul Wright*

"Lakemont" was designed and hooked by Mary Evans, student of Mary Paul Wright. The hooked rug illustrates family activity on Lake Rabun in Georgia. 40" x 55". *Photo courtesy of Mary Paul Wright*

8 In Celebration

Rug hookers past and present relish the idea of commemorating episodes in life with samples of their handiwork. Rugs have been hooked to announce births and to honor the dead; for newlyweds and for those celebrating a lifetime shared; in homage to religious beliefs and as a symbol of pride in one's heritage. Give them a reason and they will hook rugs!

Fourteen red hearts form a simple border on this hooked rug; perhaps a gift given to a loved one on Valentine's Day. Maine origins. Circa 1880. 19" x 32". *Photo courtesy of Ralph A. Ridolfino*

Janet West celebrates the small rewards of everyday living. The hooking artist's whimsical banner illustrates slices of cherry and lemon meringue pie so generously offered. 1990. 15" x 66". *Photo by John West*

The maker of this hooked mat recorded in script the Centennial Anniversary of the adoption of the Declaration of Independence. 22" x 38". *Courtesy of Pine Cone Antiques*

This graphic rug was hooked entirely from the cotton material of old United States flags. Believed to have been made to commemorate the 100th anniversary of America's Independence. 54" x 56". 1870-1880. *Private Collection Stephen Score Inc.*

Detail shows varying shades and ages of red, white and blue cotton flag fabric. *Private Collection of Stephen Score Inc.*

Commercial pattern maker, Edward Sands Frost offered his rug hooking customers this patriotic design to celebrate the Centennial. Frost pattern No. 95. Maine origins. Late 19th century. 26" x 37". *Photo courtesy of Ralph A. Ridolfino*

Only 200 copies of Pearl K. McGown's pattern "Heritage" were issued in 1976; the 200th anniversary of America's Independence. Wilma Perrin was the recipient of one of the 200 printed designs. 18" x 26". *Courtesy of Linda J. Molloy*

Halloween crepe paper inspired hooking artist Janet West to create this delightful rug. Note the four dead mice beneath the feet of the parading black cats. Hooked in 1991. 29" x 48". *Photo by John West*

Objects of our age-old superstitions were hooked by Janet West on a striped hit-or-miss background. 30" x 32". *Photo by John West*

Fashioned after a Grandma Moses painting. "Home for Thanksgiving" depicts country folk as they scurry about in preparation for the upcoming holiday. Hooked in 1952. 20" x 32". *Photo courtesy of Alan Goldstein and Judith Taylor/ Fine Arts, Fine Rugs*

Amish Country auction hooked by Dot Abbott. From a pattern. 1992. 25" x 37".

Detail of the auctioneer offering his audience an Amish quilt.

"Santa's Messenger," a Prairie Craft pattern was recently hooked by Carol Kassera. *Photo by Jeanne Edwards*

"Merry, Merry Christmas,"Yankee Peddler pattern, hooked by rug hooking teacher Meredith P. LeBeau. 14" x 26".

"Holy Family" a Joan Moshimer pattern was hooked by Katherine M. Munnis. Diameter 18". *Courtesy of her daughter, Nancy A. Kelly*

Pat Haviland hooked this Patsy Becker pattern of three Santas in 1992. 24" x 35".

"Stained Glass Nativity,"a Jane McGown Flynn pattern was hooked by rug hooking teacher Naomi Stopher in 1986. Framed with leaded stained glass. 16" x 16". *Photo courtesy of Naomi Stopher*

"O' Christmas Tree," a Prairie House pattern, was hooked by Helen M. Payne. 39" x 39". *Photo courtesy of Helen M. Payne*

Jacqueline Gutting hooked strips of wool fabric bonded with metallic fibers into the holiday mat she designed. Note the iridescent glitter of the tree's ornaments and Christmas gifts. Hooked in 1992. 20" x 36.

Pamela J. Smith designed and hooked "Sun Dance" as a symbol of pride for her native American heritage. Pamela's ancestors were from one of the great Cherokee Indian tribes that settled in Oklahoma. Diameter 54". *Photo courtesy of Pamela J. Smith*

On January 24, 1993, artist Pamela J. Smith presented "Sun Dance" to the Sun Dance Institute in Provo, Utah. The hooked piece will be displayed with the art collection in the Institute's "Screening Room." Actor Robert Redford accepted Pamela's work on behalf of the foundation. *Photo courtesy of Pamela J. Smith*

Fiber artist and rug hooking teacher Pamela J. Smith of Miami, Florida poses with a sampling of her work. *Photo by Dan Loffler*

Saguaros and lone cowboy are set against a vivid American Southwestern sunset. Hooked in Nova Scotia, Canada. Circa 1935. 26" x 39". *Courtesy of the Kent Collection*

Silver fox farming began in the Canadian Maritime Province of Prince Edward Island about 1896. The business reached its peak between 1910 and 1914. Hooked on Prince Edward Island. Circa 1920. 24" x 40". (Information and photo courtesy of the Kent Collection

Susan L. Smidt (formerly Goldberg) hooked "Transition" as a tribute to her Jewish ancestry. A simple leaf is transformed into the Star of David. Hooked in 1986. 12" x 48".

In 1991 Susan L. Smidt was inspired to hook "Transition II." 12" x 48".

Ida Bowman stands beside the Communion bench cushion hooked for the First Christian Church in Chattanooga, Tennessee. The pattern was designed by Carol Kassera, using the church liturgical colors in the hooking. Marguerite Gilliam and Nancy Lord, members of the church assisted Ida with the project. 14" x 90". *Photo courtesy of Ida Bowman*

The flowers of 48 states were hooked by Louise Covington. "National Bouquet" is an Heirloom pattern. 37" x 62". *Photo courtesy of Louise Covington*

The Ascension Lutheran Church in Charlotte, North Carolina is the proud owner of a hooked altar rug designed by the Mills-Mosseller Studio of Tryon, North Carolina. While visiting the home of Jim and Virginia Hall, newly arrived Associate Pastor Fred Klein admired the beatiful rugs that Virginia had hooked. It was suggested that the church altar would benefit from such handsome handiwork. After some research Virginia contacted the nationally recognized Mills-Mosseller Studios. Under the guidance and supervision of Mrs. Mosseller and her son, Ronald, the project began. Church members constructed a wooden frame to support the weight of the 43 square feet of monk's cloth foundation. Shuttle hooks and hand dyed wool yarns were used by the ladies of the church who started the sizable project in June of 1974. Volunteers worked in scheduled shifts on Tuesday mornings and evenings until the rug was completed. 5′ 7″ x 12′. *Photo courtesy of Virginia Hall*

Detail of the shuttle-hooked altar rug, Ascension Lutheran Church, Charlotte, North Carolina.

In the late 1960s Marion Darbe told her hooking teacher, Annie Spring that she would like to hook "The Last Supper." W. Cushing and Company was contacted and Joan Moshimer kindly drew the pattern on a monk's cloth foundation. Marion worked on the sizable project for several years but due to illness she asked Annie Spring to complete the hooking. In 1993, Annie has nearly finished the hooked reproduction. 38" x 80". *Courtesy of Marion Darbe and Annie A. Spring*

The First Ward School was the first graded school in Charlotte, North Carolina. Displayed in the school, the hooked wall hanging was designed by the students and their art teacher. It depicts the school building and history of surrounding sites from 1900 to 1985. The names of the all the principals form an interior frame. Names of prominent area families are hooked along the rug's outer edge. Berry Jones and Virginia Hall did much of the hooking with students, parents, teachers and staff contributing their time and efforts to the project. The yarn hooked rug was presented to Cleo Gullick in 1985 to commemorate the school's 85th anniversary and honor her achievements as principal. 5′ 7″ x 12′. *Courtesy of Principal Carl Flamer, First Ward School, Charlotte, North Carolina and Virginia Hall*

Detail of the First Ward School hooked rug. Street cars were used in the area from 1911 until the early 1940s.

Detail of the First Ward School hooked rug. The house pictured was built around 1860 from heart pine. Three generations of one family lived and died in this home.

Detail of the First Ward School hooked rug. The top building is the Afro-American Cultural Center. The center structures are "Shotgun Houses." If one stood in the front yard of these early rental homes, a shot could be fired through the front door and exit through the back door without causing any damage. These two houses were moved, restored and are now maintained by the Afro-American Cultural Center in Charlotte. The building below is the Alexander Hotel. Before integration, this was the only hotel open to Afro-Americans and was a popular social place for hosting entertainers, professionals and for occasions of importance.

Hooked coffin rugs were made by family members and placed upon the casket of a departed loved one. The handiwork was often a substitute for a traditional display of fresh flowers. The rug pictured was hooked by Alma Hilliard about 1870 and remains in the possession of her granddaughter, Grace Hilliard Barker. 44" x 72". *Courtesy of Grace H. Barker*

Detail of the coffin rug hooked by Alma Hilliard. In addition to the Cross and floral wreath, she hooked a pair of doves, each bearing an olive branch.

A sorrowful widow hooked this rug to commemorate her three departed husbands, Paul, Henry and Tony. The pulled back blue curtain indicates that perhaps she could view their graves from her window. A weeping willow bends its branches over the burial sight. Circa 1900. 37" x 48".

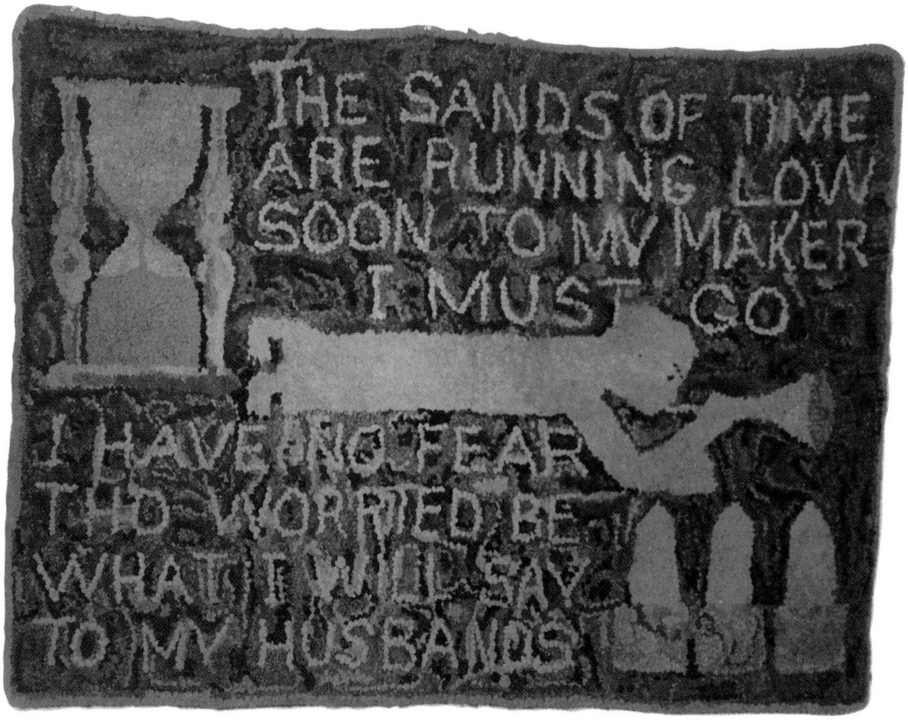
THE SANDS OF TIME
ARE RUNNING LOW
SOON TO MY MAKER
I MUST GO
I HAVE NO FEAR
THO WORRIED BE
WHAT I WILL SAY
TO MY HUSBANDS

One begins to wonder about the character of the thrice widowed woman who hooked this commemorative rug. Did her three husbands die of natural causes? Circa 1890. *Courtesy of Stephen Score Inc.*

"Blue Angel,"designed and recently hooked by Jeanne Fallier. 16" x20". *Photo courtesy of Jeanne Fallier*

9 Passing on the Tradition

Ramona Maddox

Below the Mason/Dixon Line in the historically rich city of Chattanooga, Tennessee lives a rug hooking teacher who serves as an inspiration to all others with the same calling. Ramona Maddox's enthusiasm for creating beautiful floor coverings from strips of wool is contagious. Her zealousness for the craft she loves is felt by all who have the pleasure of meeting this gracious lady.

Ramona studied rug hooking under the tutelage of Phyllis Regan and in 1973 became a certified McGown teacher. During 1930's and 1940's Pearl McGown, a native of Massachusetts, was instrumental in reviving an interest in rug hooking. The methods she taught are still being used in 1993. Teachers who earn a McGown accreditation are counted among the best in the rug hooking world.

Today Ramona maintains a full schedule as a much-demanded hooking teacher for the Chattanooga Hookrafters. She is President of the National Pearl K. McGown Guild and travels across the United States to address its many members.

Hooking artist and teacher Ramona Maddox poses at her rug frame. *Photo by Bob Nichols—Chattanooga Free Press*

Rugs hooked under the guidance of Ramona Maddox are scattered throughout this book. Pictured is Kathleen Crowe, one of Ramona's many students. She works on "Persian Magic,"a Pearl K. McGown pattern. 5′ 6″ x 8′. *Photo courtesy Ramona Maddox*

Hooked reproduction of Leonardo da Vinci's "The Last Supper" by Ramona Maddox. 38" x 80". *Photo courtesy of Ramona Maddox*

A paneled screen of Oriental vases was designed and hooked by Ramona Maddox. 5' 5" x 12' 9". *Photo courtesy of Ramona Maddox*

Detail of the Christ figure shows the subtle changes of color used by Ramona.

"Persian Minature,"a Pearl K. McGown pattern, was hooked by Ramona Maddox. 4' 2" x 5' 3". *Photo courtesy of Ramona Maddox*

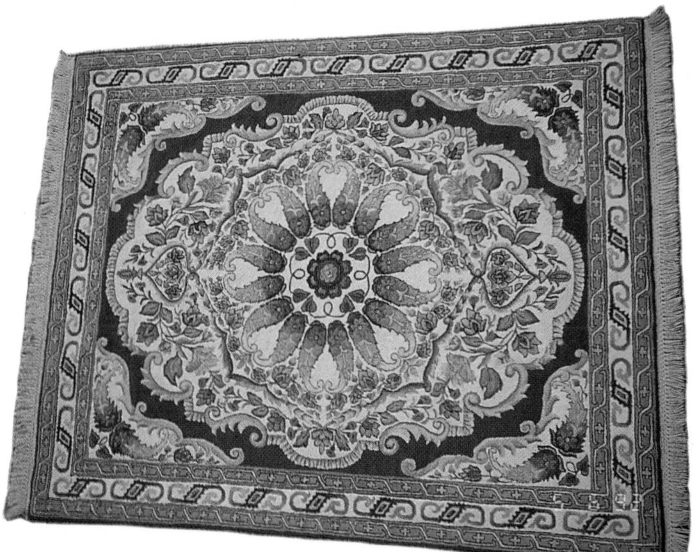

Since 1976, Castle In The Clouds rug hooking school has been held at Covenant College, high atop Lookout Mountain in Chattanooga, Tennessee. Each May, the school's founder and chief organizer Ramona Maddox employs a variety of talented instructors, and offers rug hooking seminars to a growing roster of eager students. Reminiscent of boarding pupils that attend Covenant College during the academic year, rug hookers and their teachers arrive lugging crammed suitcases, balancing rugs frames, stacks of burlap and bolts of wool material.

Students receive a full five days of intense instruction covering all aspects of rug hooking from start to finish. Three meals a day and sleeping accommodations are available on the college campus. An exhibit of past and present projects is open to the public. The Castle In The Clouds class of 1992 numbered over 100 with participants traveling from as far as Texas, Maine, Florida and Illinois, joined by local hookrafters who have not missed the annual event since its conception in 1976.

In 1984 the Chattanooga Choo-Choo Conference Center hosted the biennial National McGown Guild Exhibit. In April, 1992, windows of the Blue Cross and Blue Shield building in downtown Chattanooga came alive with a colorful display of rugs hooked by the women and men who study with Ramona. And in May of each year the Hookrafters sponsor an exhibit at Covenant College in conjunction with the annual Castle in the Clouds Rug Hooking School. Ramona Maddox and her loyal band of Hookrafters have played a crucial role in promoting rug hooking in the South. Such dedication is rare.

Covenant College, Chattanooga, Tennessee; site of Castle In The Clouds rug hooking school. *Photo courtesy of Ramona Maddox*

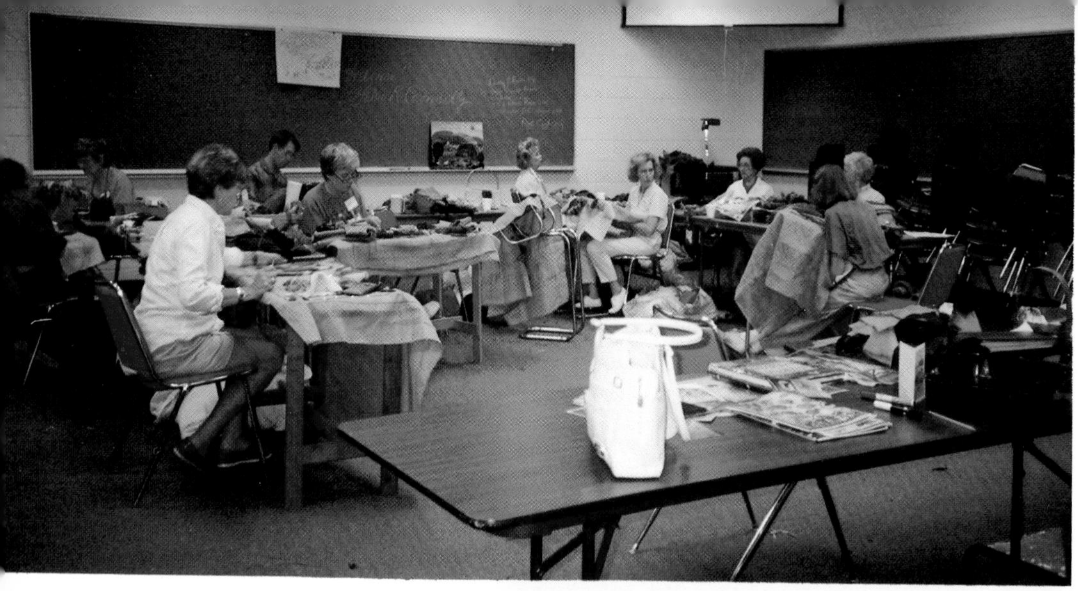

One of the many class rooms filled with eager rug hookers at Castle In The Clouds. May 1992. *Photo courtesy of Ramona Maddox*

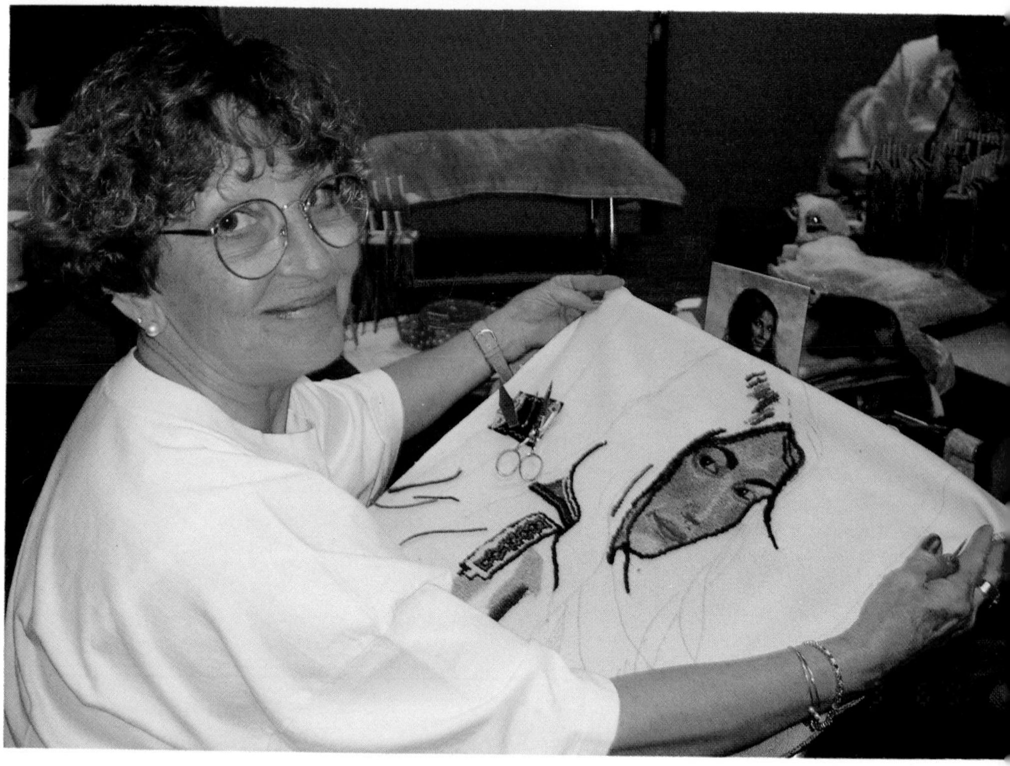

Barbara Pritle traveled from Indiana to attend Ramona Maddox's rug hooking school. She works on "Stronghold Princess", portrait of an Indian girl. *Photo by Jeanne Edwards*

After five days of study and hard work, Ramona Maddox invites all rug hooking students and teachers to an old fashioned Tennessee riverboat cruise. Fine dining and live music are enjoyed by all. Pictured in lavender is Ramona Maddox; to her left, husband Owen; to her right, rug hooking friends Ralph and Mavis Williams. *Photo by Jeanne Edwards*

10 All Creatures Great and Small

When hooking an animal motif, early rug makers most often drew a dog, cat or horse upon their burlap or homespun foundation. Domesticated animals were the recipients of love and respect from their owners, deemed worthy of being portrayed in a rug should a member of the household be talented in the craft of hooking. The animal rugs hooked during the mid to late 1800s were often crude and childlike. An enduring folk art charm has made them most desireable to collectors. Animal hooked rugs of significant age are scarce. In the late 1860s Edward Sands Frost began to print and sell burlap patterns for rug hooking. Frost realized the great admiration that owners had for their pets and offered dog, cat and horse designs. With a bit of artistic ability, the generic animal patterns could be hooked to resemble one's own Fido, Puss or Lightning.

Those creatures outside the realm of the barnyard and forest remained foreign to the majority of men and women hooking rugs in the late 1800s. Exotic animals were viewed through artists' renderings or seen if and when the circus came to town. With the exception of a popular hooked rug pattern of a mighty lion, attributed to both Frost and his competitor Ebeneezer Ross, and a design of a leopard-like creature, the number of rugs depicting exotic animals is small.

As the world grows smaller due to the advancements in technology, those beasts once strange to our departed ancestors' eyes are everyday images for us, with our television sets, movies, books and zoos. Today, all creatures great and small are potential candidates for a hooked rug portrait.

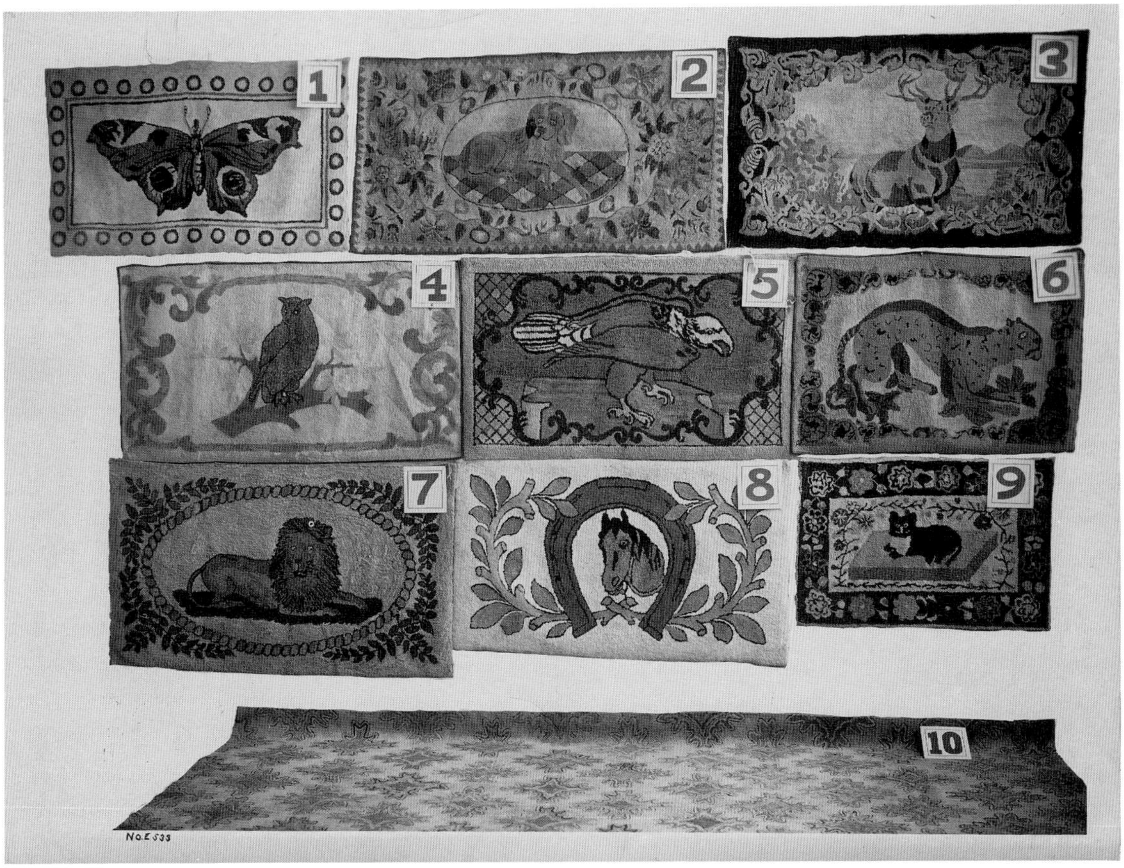

In the early 1900s, Ralph W. Burham, antiques dealer from Ipswich, Massachusetts offered a selection of animal motif hooked rugs for sale. The grouping includes several Frost patterns. *Courtesy of Annie A. Spring*

Believed to be one of the rarest examples of early folk art in the Burnham collection of hooked rugs. Crafted from clothing of Revolutionary War soldiers. Note the enlarged flowers growing from the tree. Horses, birds and a single cat are included in the design. 1850-1870. *Courtesy of Annie A. Spring*

Velvet handbag from England with needlepoint and hooked insert. The wreath of leaves and dogs with rabbit were hooked and sculptured with woolen yarns. The Burnham Collection. Circa 1890. 14" x 15". *Courtesy of Annie A. Spring*

A Stubbs painting inspired artist Joan Moshimer's hooked portrait of King Charles' spaniels. 1991. 23" x 50". *Photo by Robert Moshimer*

Betsy Adams Church hooks a likeness of Molly, her golden retriever.

The wool portrait of Molly was Betsy Adams Church's first attempt at rug hooking. She designed the rug and dyed much of wool material used. 1993. 30" x 40".

Mary Perry memorialized four favorite pets in her hooked rug. A combination of as-is and hand-dyed wool material are being used to create the outdoor scene. 1993.

Raised and sculptured roses form a border around the German shepherd designed and hooked by Jacqueline Hansen. 1989.

An inquisitive Siamese cat was hooked by Mary Hargrove. DiFranza pattern. Diameter 14". *Photo courtesy of Mary Hargrove*

"Ashley Wilkes,"a favorite feline friend was portrayed in a hooked mat designed and worked by Faye Jackson. 1987. 25" x 27". *Photo courtesy of Faye Jackson*

A pair of cats try their skill at the game of dominoes. Circa 1880. 24" x 40". *Courtesy of Bert and Carol Rosengarten*

"Persian Blue," hooked by Joan Moshimer. 1990. 27" x 27". *Photo by Robert Moshimer*

Hallie H. Hall hooked her own interpretation of a whimsical antique rug. 1980s. 28" x 37".

A hooked cat in the making by Ethel Bruce. Pearl K. McGown pattern.

Susan Morin utilizes her hooked rug as a fire screen. Jane McGown Flynn pattern. 1990. *Photo courtesy of Susan Morin.*

The edges of hooked rugs are generally the first area to show wear. Sturdy braids were often added to the rug for protection from further damage. Frost pattern. Maine origins. Circa 1900. 28" x 36". *Courtesy of Thomas M. Thompson Antiques*

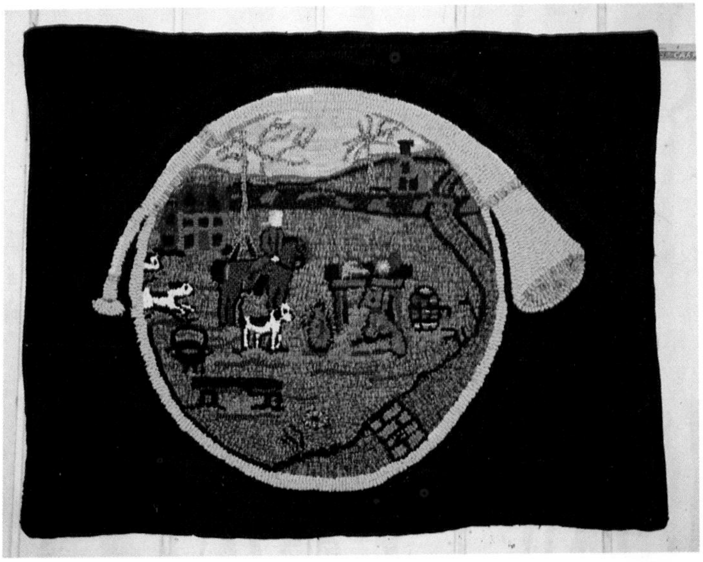

"Morning Hunt" was designed and hooked by Faye Jackson. 1991. 26" x 35". *Photo courtesy of Faye Jackson*

Artist Cindy Thompson hooked her entire composition from the fabric of old riding jackets. *Photo courtesy of Cindy Thompson*

Both cow and background were hooked in patch-work shades of color. Circa 1890. 29″ x 46″.
Private Collection

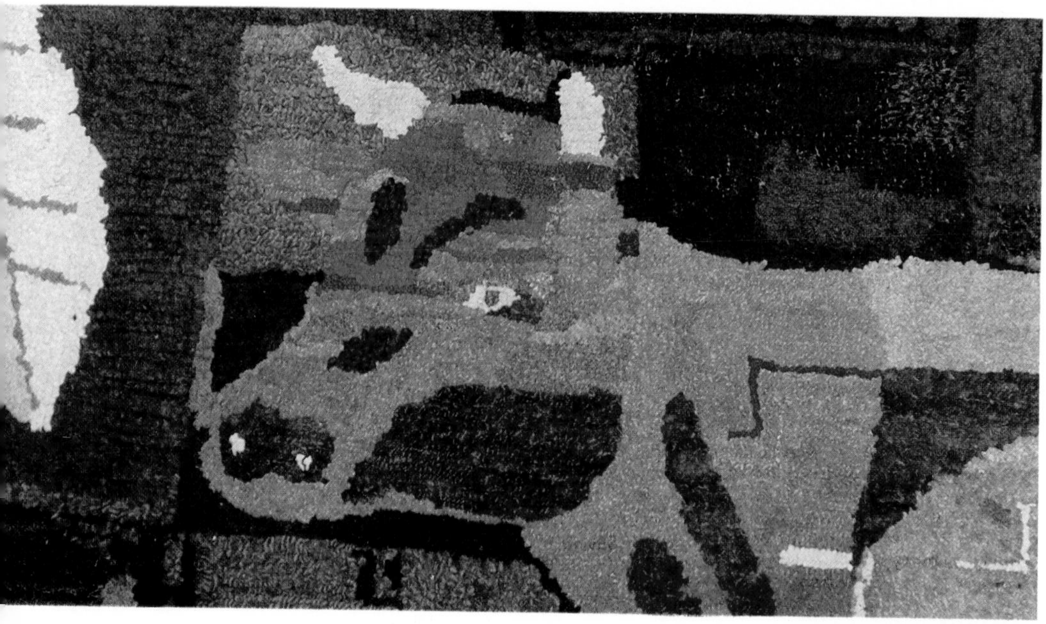

Detail shows the variety of textiles used to hook the cow rug.

"Rosebud," designed and hooked by Mary Evans. 30″ x 37″.
Photo courtesy of Mary Evans

Believed to be hooked by the Amish in Lancaster County, Pennsylvania. 1910-1920. 18" x 34". ***Courtesy of*** *Mary Carden Quinn*

"Lamb,"designed and hooked by Cindy Thompson. 24" x 24". *Photo courtesy of Cindy Thompson*

Detail of a sheep hooked by Hallie H. Hall. Jane McGown Flynn pattern

"Buffalo" designed and hooked by Cindy Thompson. 30" x 39". *Photo courtesy of Cindy Thompson*

"Bunny Heaven" hooked by Sue Stopher. Patsy Becker pattern. 1981-1982. 24" x 40". *Photo courtesy of Sue Stopher*

Anthony Travis took up the craft of hooking while recuperating from knee and hip replacement surgery. Though literally back on his feet again, he continues to hook rugs. 1993. 21" x 30".

Adaptation of Beatrix Potter's *Peter Rabbit*, hooked by Connie Fletcher. 1991. 20" x 24". *Photo courtesy of Connie Fletcher*

"Little Bandit," hooked by Naomi Stopher. Jane McGown Flynn pattern. 1983. 14" x 18". *Photo courtesy of Naomi Stopher*

Adapted from a photograph found in *The National Geographic of Wild Animals of North America*. Hooked by Faith Henshall. 30" x 50". *Photo courtesy of Faith Henshall*

Deers in the woodland from the Burnham Collection. Circa 1880. 31" x 61". *Courtesy of Annie A. Spring*

An unusual and rare example of a hooked mat made by the Grenfell Industries in Labrador and Newfoundland. The majority of Grenfell mats sold by the mission were hooked from patterns printed with Northern themes. The rose wreath and vases of assorted flowers are unique. This was most likely a one-of-a-kind artistic attempt by a creative mat maker. Early 20th century. *Private Collecton of Stephen Score Inc.*

Rug hooking teacher and artist Annie A. Spring holds the wall hanging she hooked. The composition, inspired by a photograph, was awarded first prize at the Women's International Exposition in New York City during 1960. 23" x 27".

Tropical parrots are the subject of this unusual antique rug. Circa 1880. 35" x 65". *Courtesy of the Estate of Mary Rachel Scott and the Private Collection of Jane Torrance Baker*

Inspired by a photograph from *The National Geographic of Wild Animals of North America*. Hooked by Faith Henshall. 44" x 60". *Photo courtesy of Faith Henshall*

Frost pattern of a parrot-like bird. From the Burnham Collection. Circa 1890. *Courtesy of Annie A. Spring*

Designed and hooked by Jacqueline Hansen. The parrot, floral sprays and border motif are raised and sculptured in a manner similar to rugs hooked in the Waldoboro, Maine area during the second half of the 1800s. 1989. 20" x 30".

A fierce looking eagle observes all from his lofty perch. The fabric loops that form the eagle's body were hooked slightly higher than the background to give added dimension to the bird. Circa 1900. 37" x 52". *Courtesy of Donna A. Terzian*

A wonderful folk art, hearth size rug with acorns, stars, hearts, plants and birds. Rhode Island origins. Circa 1860. *Private Collection of Stephen Score Inc.*

"Birds and Fish," designed and hooked by Mary Mann. 1991. 20" x 30". *Photo courtesy of Mary Mann*

"Heron" hooked by Ruth Roccia. Adaptation of a Jane McGown Flynn pattern. The design was fashioned after tapestries owned by The Metropolitan Museum of Art in New York and exhibited at the Cloisters. Completed in 1992. 24" x 35". *Photo courtesy of Ruth Roccia*

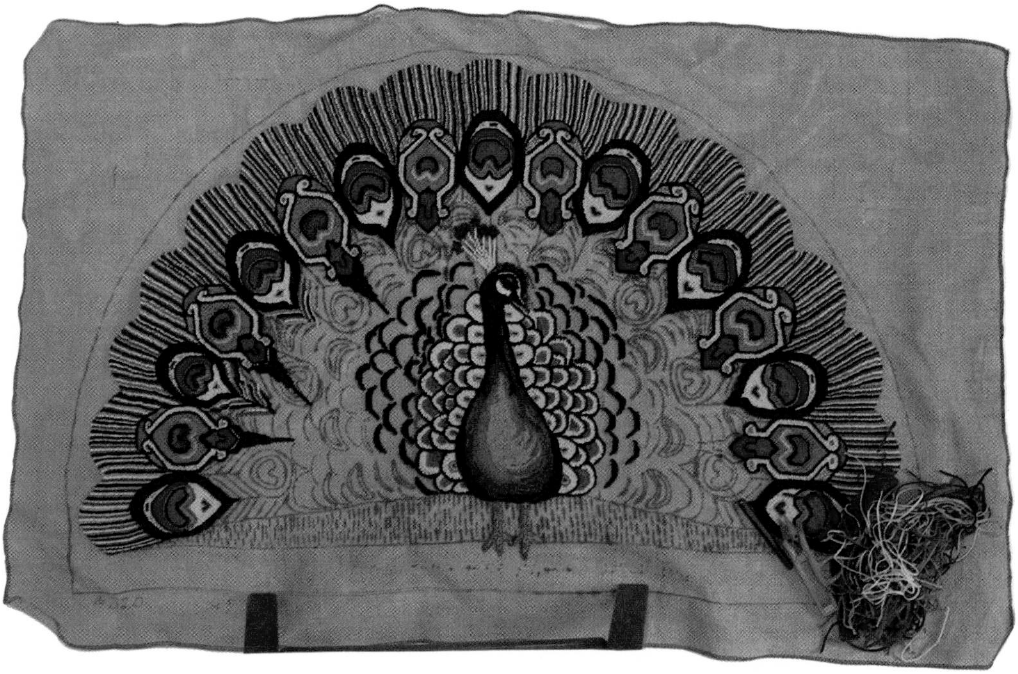

Wendy Ullmann is in the process of hooking an elaborate peacock. Joan Moshimer pattern modified with an Oriental accent.

"The Crane,"a copy of an antique rug was hooked by Diane LeGros. Lib Callaway pattern. 30" x 51". *Photo courtesy of Diane LeGros / Southern Traditions-Custom Primitive Hand-Hooked Rugs*

"Freedom" hooked by Faith Henshall. Pearl K. McGown pattern. Completed in 1979. 30" x 50". *Photo courtesy of Faith Henshall*

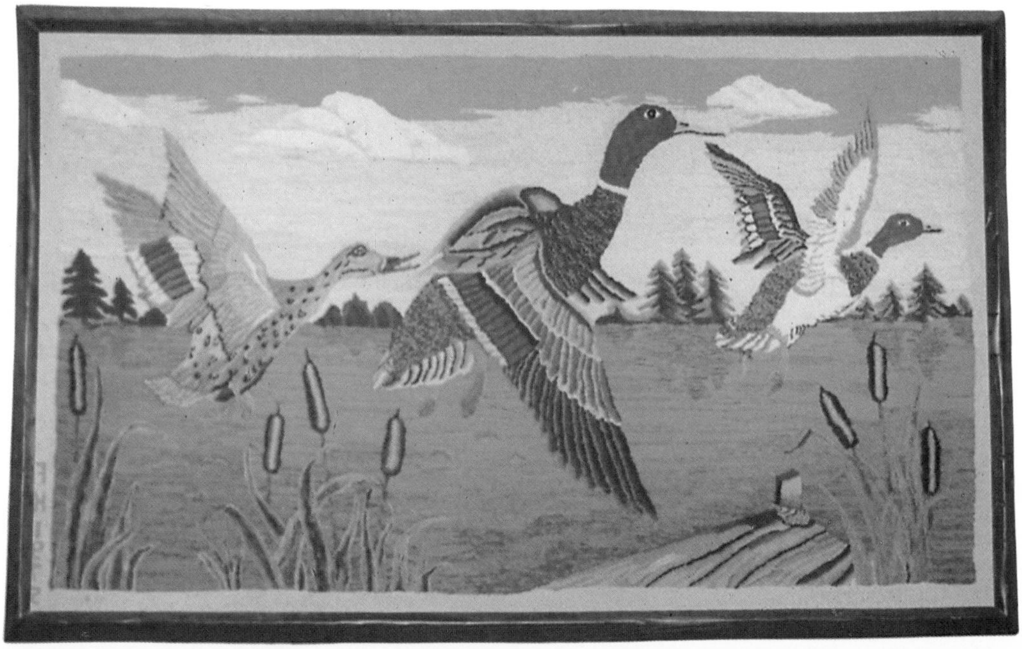

"25 Chickens and One Worm,"adapted from a quilt pattern and hooked by Naomi Stopher. 30" x 44". *Photo courtesy of Naomi Stopher*

"Sea Shells and Pelicans,"hooked by Pat Fletcher. 1991. Diameter 36". *Photo by Jeanne Edwards*

Faye A. Gilman used a black and white plaid wool material to hook this hen. 13" x 17". *Photo courtesy of Faye A. Gilman*

"Penguins,"hooked by Cindy Thompson. Adapted from a photograph in *National Geographic*. 20" x 50". *Photo courtesy of Cindy Thompson*

"Puffins at Home,"designed and hooked by Jeanne Fallier. 1985. 20" x 30". *Photo courtesy of Jeanne Fallier*

A butterfly wall-hanging hooked by Hallie H. Hall in the 1970s.

"Jolly Lions,"hooked by Wendy Meredith. Lib Callaway pattern. *Photo courtesy of Wendy Meredith*

"Tree of Life,"hooked by Richard Scott. Yankee Peddler pattern. 38" x 51". *Photo courtesy of Richard Scott*

An Oriental screen inspired Dot Loney to create her own hooked version. The design was printed on homespun by rug hooking teacher Jacqueline Hansen of Scarborough, Maine. The wool materials used to hook with were hand-dyed by rug hooking teacher Ramona Maddox of Chattanooga, Tennessee. With Ramona's guidance, Dot hooked the individual panels. 30" x 72". *Photo courtesy of Dot Loney*

"The Tiger Rugs of Tibet" exhibit held at the Hayward Gallery in London during 1988 inspired artist Janet West to hook her own tiger skin rug. 1989. 37" x 61" *Photo by John West*

"Sandy's Lion," hooked by Naomi Stopher in monochromatic tones. Jane McGown Flynn pattern. 14" x 1 6". *Photo courtesy of Naomi Stopher*

"Leopard Oval," designed and hooked by Marion N. Ham. 36" x 50". *Photo courtesy of Marion N. Ham*

"Jonah," designed and hooked by artist Cindy Thompson. 24" x 36". *Photo courtesy of Cindy Thompson*

A magazine cover inspired Bernice Bickum to hook this playful chimpanzee. 12" x 16". *Courtesy of Renee M. Goldberg*

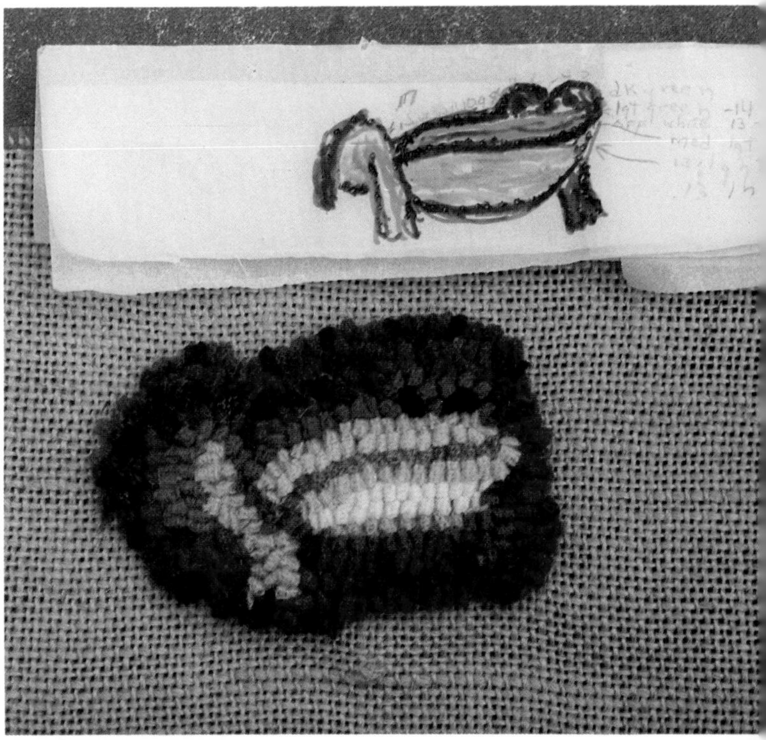

Betty Supple created a whimsical little frog by hooking only a few lines of color. 1993.

"Dolphins," designed and hooked by Jeanne Fallier. 1991. 24" x 36". *Photo courtesy of Jeanne Fallier*

"Fish Ladder," designed and hooked by Jeanne Fallier. Inspiration for the pattern came after a visit to the fish ladder at Columbia Gorge in Oregon. 22" x 30". Photo courtesy of Jeanne Fallier

"Carp," designed and hooked by Majorie Noon. 1986. 30" x 39".

"Farm and Forest" hooked by Betty Supple for her grandaughter Lydia. Joan Moshimer pattern. 1992-1993. 24" x 36".

Detail of Betty Supple's hooked rug.

"Adam and Eve,"designed by Barbara Brown and hooked by Mary Floyd. 1990. 20″ x 27″. *Photo courtesy of Mary Floyd*

"Adam and Eve" surrounded by endangered species was designed and hooked by artist Cindy Thompson. 1992. 30″ x 30″. *Photo courtesy of Cindy Thompson*

"Children's Portrait,"designed by Ed Gilliam and hooked by Sandy Gilliam. The Gilliam's four children are pictured with their favorite animals. Family home and nearby lake are in the background. Children's names and birth dates frame the rug. *Photo courtesy of Sandy Gilliam*

"Noah's Ark,"an adaptation of a Charles Wysoki calendar drawing. Hooked by Georgia Kimball. 1989. 39" x 49". *Photo courtesy of Georgia Kimball*

"Freddie's Safari,"designed and hooked by Phyllis Perry for her grandson. 45" x 54". *Photo courtesy of Phyllis Perry*

Hooking artist Janet West's first rug was a menagerie of whimsical animals. 1988. 32" x 46". *Photo by John West*

"Stones" designed and hooked by Phyllis Perry. A favorite beach in Tortola, British Virgin Islands was the inspiration for her composition. 28" x 43". *Photo courtesy of Phyllis Perry*

During the summer of 1989, Nova Scotia rug hooker Muriel Peveril received a telephone call from Massachusetts. Mrs. Pinkham was searching for someone to hook her a rug. Years before, friend and artist Nan Lee had drawn a pattern depicting the "Peaceable Kingdom" at the request of Margaret Pinkham. Margaret had given Nan a large piece of monk's cloth assuming she would use only a small section. Nan Lee delivered a 10′ x 14′ design. Knowing that she was unable to hook such a big rug, the pattern was put away by Mrs. Pinkham. Fifteen years later, after many unsuccessful attempts to locate someone to hook the large rug, Margaret Pinkham was directed to Muriel Peveril. With the encouragement of her husband, Muriel accepted the enormous undertaking and the pattern was brought to Nova Scotia. Large amounts of wool were ordered and hand-dyed. For one year, Muriel worked diligently on the rug. In August of 1990, the finished product was delivered to the Pinkham's home. Currently the "Peaceable Kingdom" rug is on display in the meditation room of the chapel of Trinity University in San Antonio, Texas. 10′ x 14′. *Photo courtesy of Muriel Peveril*

Artist Nan Lee designed and drew the pattern for the "Peaceable Kingdom" rug on a monk's cloth foundation. She also planned the color scheme for the composition. *Photo courtesy of Margaret Pinkham*

Detail of the "Peaceable Kingdom" rug.

Muriel Peveril stands beside the nearly completed "Peaceable Kingdom" rug. Few rugs of this size are ever started; even less are ever finished. The accomplishment of such an overwhelming project attests to Muriel's skill and dedication as a rug hooking artist. *Photo courtesy of Muriel Peveril*

11 Nature's Bounty

Rug makers enjoy hooking a bountiful harvest of fruits and vegetables. All of nature's best comes to life through the skill of hand and hook. Generally rug workers allow for liberties with the colors they choose to hook. Images of summer roses have been fashioned from shades of blue. Such coloring is not found in any garden, but the unnatural tint is of no concern to its creator.

However, rugs that depict fruits and vegetables are almost always hooked in true-to-life colors. Extra time and effort is taken to select and dye fabrics for the rugs that pay hommage to the farmer's labor.

Hooking rugs with vegetable and fruit motifs became popular in the 1930's and 1940's and continues through present day. Cornucopias overflowing with garden produce add charm to the dining area of any home.

Eight shades of wool were used to hook these life-like apples.

Hallie H. Hall stands before a sampling of the wool she dyes and hooks.

New Hampshire rug hooking artist and teacher Hallie H. Hall reproduced a Peale still life of fruit. She achieved the likeness of an oil painting with her shaded wool. 1980s. 19" x 29".

Detail shows the variety of shaded wool used by the hooking artist.

An unfinished hooked rug of cornucopias overflowing with fruits and vegetables. The project is the combined effort of Grace N. O'Neil and Betty McClentic. 8′ 6″ x 11′ 6″.

Detail illustrates hooked fruits and vegetables that could stimulate one's appetite.

Ethel Fitzgerald, aunt of the late actor Rock Hudson has enjoyed the craft of hooking for over forty years. During the 1980s she worked this room size, oval shaped rug of summer fruits. Hooked from a pattern. 7′ 6″ x 10′.

Ethel Fitzgerald hooked a threshold mat to compliment her large fruit rug. Joan Moshimer pattern. 1980s. 25″ x 40″.

Jean Jones displays her hooked art in a gilt frame. Pearl K. McGown pattern. Diameter 14″.

Betty Maley hand-dyed the colors for her fruit rug using white and pastel wool. Jane McGown Flynn pattern. 1985. Diameter 36".

Detail of Betty Maley's hooked rug shows the subtle changes of color used for shading fruit.

Betty McHugh of Georgia hooked and sculptured a wreath of fruits, pine cones and foliage. *Photo courtesy of Betty McHugh*

A brick covered with hooked strawberries makes a charming doorstop. Hooked by Meredith P. LeBeau. Jane McGown Flynn pattern. 5" x 9".

"Della Robbia Wreath" was hooked by Ethel Bruce, rug hooking teacher from Massachusetts. Jane McGown Flynn pattern. 16" x 16".

Detail of a fruit and vegetable rug hooked by teacher Meredith P. LeBeau.

Opposite Page, Top Left:
Rug hooking teacher and niece of "Hooked Rug Magnate" Ralph W. Burnham, Annie A. Spring won second prize in 1960 for her sculptured fruit chair pad. The work was exhibited in at the Women's International Exposition in New York City. Karlkraft pattern. 16" x 18".

A teacher's sampler of fruits, flowers and foliage was hooked by Meredith P. LeBeau in 1985. Jane McGown Flynn pattern. 20" x 38".

Earl C. Majors enjoys hooking the patterns printed on burlap food and grain sacks. 20" x 24". *Photo courtesy of Earl C. Majors.*

Annie A. Spring hooked the same Karlkraft pattern with a black background. 15 " x 16".

Carolyn Watt fashioned the first rug she hooked after a theorem painting. The background color was obtained by dyeing white wool fabric with the skins of yellow onions. 1991-1992. 29" x 47".

Detail of Carolyn Watt's rug shows subtleties of an onion skin dyed background against the basket of colorful fruit.

"Caswell Fruit" was hooked by Laura Coppinger. Marion N. Ham pattern. 1988-1989. 42" x 72". *Photo courtesy of Laura Coppinger*

Mary Williamson hooked "Bountiful Bowl." Jane McGown Flynn pattern. 18" x 30". *Photo courtesy of Mary Williamson*

Celia Gutting works at shading a hooked apple.

Rug hooking is new to Sandy Wilder. For her first project she chose a small mat with fruit design.

12 Selected Reading

Batchhelder, Martha. *The Art of Hooked Rug Making*. Peoria, Illinois: The Manual Arts Press, 1947.

Beatty, Alice and Mary Sargent. *The Hook Book*. Harrisburg, Pennsylvania: Stackpole Books, 1975.

Blanford, William B. and Elizabeth Blanford, *Beauport Impressions*. Boston: The Society of the Preservation of New England Antiquities, 1965.

Boswell, Thom. *The Rug Hook Book*. New York: Sterling Publishing Co., Inc., 1992.

Bowles, Ella Shannon. *Handmade Rugs*. New York: Garden City Publishing., Inc., 1937.

Field, Jeanne. *Shading Flowers, The Complete Guide for Rug Hookers. Harrisburg, Pennslyvania: Stackpole Books, 1991.*

Frost, Edward Sands. Hooked Rug Patterns. Dearborn, Michigan: Greenfield Village and Henry Ford Museum, 1970.

Gallagher, Hugh Gregory. *FDR's Splendid Deception*. New York: Dodd, Mead and Co., 1985.

Kent, William Winthrop. *The Hooked Rug*. New York: Tudor Publishing Co., 1930.

Kent, William Winthrop. *Hooked Rug Design*. Springfield, Massachusetts: The Pond-Ekberg Company, 1949.

Kent, William Winthrop. *Rare Hooked Rugs*. Springfield, Massachusetts: The Pond-Ekbeg Company, 1941.

Kopp, Joel and Kate. *American Hooked and Sewn Rugs*. New York: E. P. Dutton Inc., 1975.

Linsley, Leslie, *Hooked Rugs, An American Folk Art*. New York: Clarkson Potter/Publishers, 1992.

McGown, Pearl K. *Color in Hooked Rugs*. Boston: Buck Printing Co., 1954.

McGown, Pearl K. Dreams Beneath the Design. Boston: Bruce Humphries Inc., 1939.

McGown, Pearl K. *The Lore and Lure of Hooked Rugs*. Acton, Massachusetts: Acton Press, 1966.

McGown, Pearl K. *You...Can Hook Rugs*. Boston: Buck Printing Co., 1951.

Moshimer, Joan. *The Complete Rug Hooker*. Boston: New York Graphic Society, 1975.

Moshimer, Joan. *Hooked on Cats*. Harrisburg, Pennsylvania: Stackpole Books. 1991.

Phillips, Anna M. Laise. *Hooked Rugs and How To Make Them*. New York: The MacMillan Co., 1925.

Rex, Stella Hay. *Practical Hooked Rugs*. Asheville, Maine: Cobblesmith, 1975.

Ries, Estelle H. *American Rugs*. Cleveland, Ohio: The World Publishing Co., 1950.

Stratton, Charlotte Kimball. *Rug Hooking Made Easy. New York: Harper and Brothers Publishers, 1955.*

Taylor, Mary Perkins. How To Make Hooked Rugs. Philadelphia: David McKay Publishers, 1930.

Turbayne, Jessie A. *Hooked Rugs, History and The Continuing Tradition*. West Chester, Pennsyvania: Schiffer Publishing, Ltd., 1991.

Underhill, Vera Bisbee with Arhur J. Burks. *Creating Hooked Rugs*. New York: Coward-McCann, 1951.

Waugh, Elizabeth and Edith Foley. *Collecting Hooked Rugs*. New York: The Century Co., 1927.

"Aunt Meg,"a copy of an antique rug, was hooked by Sandy Heino. Heirloom pattern. 36" x 59".

13 Price Guide

Establishing a price guide for hooked rugs is difficult. Whether an original composition or worked from a printed pattern, every hooked piece is a reflection of the person that created it. Each hooked rug needs to be judged on an individual basis.

The cost to have a rug custom designed and hooked can range anywhere from $50 per square foot to $150 per square foot. Price is effected by the amount of hand dyeing required to satisfy color needs and the fineness of the loops hooked. The thinner the strips of wool are cut, the longer it takes to hook an area. Intricate patterns and shading with several colors add to the hooking time and expense. Be aware that there are few individuals that will hand-hook a rug for a per square foot fee. The majority of rugs hooked today are done for the love of the craft. They are rarely sold.

Prices for antique and semi-antique hooked rugs are wide and varied. Age, condition, subject matter and size all affect the monetary value of old hooked rugs. Costs can range anywhere from a few dollars for an antique rug in poor condition to tens of thousands of dollars for a pristine example of early (1860-1880) hooked folk art.

Most sought-after are one-of-a-kind animal rugs at least 100 years old. These are scarce and generally command high prices. Grenfell mats, hooked in Newfoundland and Labrador during the early 1900s, are among the highest-priced older hooked pieces. Sold by the mission to aid Dr. Grenfell's medical and social work, the finely hooked mats depict Northern themes such as polar bears, icebergs and dog teams. Prices for Grenfell mats in good condition can range from $100 to $4000. Those in need of repair are priced accordingly.

Antique hooked rugs of geometric, floral, pictorial or Oriental design have also risen in value. As the demand for old hooked rugs increases, the supply dwindles. Room-size rugs and lengthy stair runners are scarce, and therefore prices paid for hooked rugs of sizable measurements reflect their availability.

In the past ten years I have seen a steady increase in sales and prices for rugs hooked during the 1930s and 1940s. Most popular during this period were elaborate floral patterns framed by twisting scrolls. Prices for rugs of this vintage in good condition can start at $100 and climb to thousands of dollars. Artistic quality, condition and size are important factors when purchasing a hooked rug that is 40 to 60 years old.

Hooking is now widely acknowledged as a true art form. The price for today's hooked art is being established by recognized hooking artists such as Roslyn Logsdon, Mary Sheppard Burton, Fumiyo Hachisuka and others. Original hooked works of art are being exhibited at galleries and museums across the United States and internationally.

Wenham Cross Antiques in Boston, Massachusetts offers an interesting selection of hooked and braided rugs. *Photo courtesy of Wenham Cross Antiques*

Antique shows are a good place to buy hooked rugs. Pictured is the booth of James A. and Jessie A. Turbayne. Brimmer and May Antique Show, Chestnut Hill, Massachusetts. 1992. The hooked rugs displayed are of varying vintages. *Photos by Robert H. Kurtz*

The Boston Antiques Show sponsored by the Boys and Girls Clubs of Boston, Inc. 1992. Booth of Wellington Guild and James A. Turbayne. The large, hanging rug was hooked in the 1940s and measures 7′ 6″ x 9′ 5″.

An early cupboard holds hooked rugs of varying ages.

Ellen Youlden has been hooking for over twenty years. She works at carefully shading the flowers she hooks.

Close-up of "Patrician", hooked by Annie A. Spring. Pearl K. McGown pattern.

Index

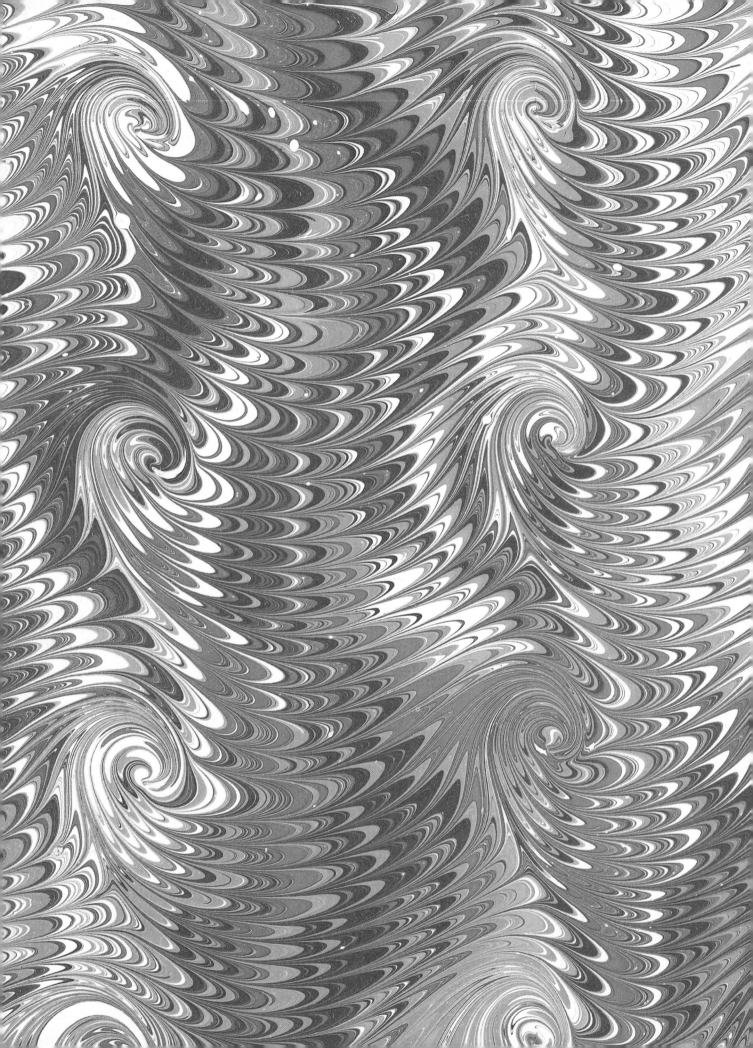